7 DIMENSIONS & OPERATIONS of the Kingdom of God

ABRAHAM JOHN

7 Dimensions and Operations of the Kingdom of God

Kingdom Secrets to Restoring Nations Back to God, Vol. 11

Copyright © 2018 by Abraham John

Published by Abraham John

www.TheKingdomNetwork.org
email: info@thekingdomnetwork.org
1-800-558-5020
(720)-560-4664

ISBN: 978-1-948330-15-2

Printed in the United States of America

Unless otherwise indicated, all Scripture taken from the New King James Version®. Copyright © 1982 by Thomas Nelson. Used by permission.

Scripture marked (KJV) is from the King James Version of the Bible, which is in the public domain.

All *emphasis* or additions in parentheses within scriptural quotations are the author's own.

All rights reserved. No part of this book may be reproduced or transmitted in any form or by any means, electronic or mechanical, including photocopying, recording, or by any information storage and retrieval system, without permission in writing from the author. Please direct your inquiries to mim@maximpact.org

Table of Contents

Preface		5
Introduction		11
Chapter 1	Sevenfold Transition	19
Chapter 2	Understanding God's Order	45
Chapter 3	Dimension 1: God's Eternal Kingdom	63
Chapter 4	Dimension 2: The Kingdom of God in the Garden of Eden	75
Chapter 5	Dimension 3: Kingdom of God through the Lives of the Patriarchs	93
Chapter 6	Dimension 4: Kingdom of God through the Nation of Israel	111
Chapter 7	Dimension 5: Kingdom of God that came with the first coming of Jesus Christ	119
Chapter 8	Kingdom of God in the Four Gospels	127
Chapter 9	Dimension 6: Kingdom of God in the Church Age	145
Chapter 10	The Book of Acts from a Kingdom Perspective	153
Chapter 11	Dimension 7: Kingdom of God During the Millennial Reign and Beyond	171
Chapter 12	The Present Kingdom	175
More Books & Resources		181

Preface

God has revealed His purpose and plan for the earth and spoken to the human race in a variety of ways since the beginning of time. At this end time, He has revealed His will through His Son Jesus Christ and through His holy apostles and prophets. Jesus spoke about the kingdom of God more than any other subject. In the Bible we see God's kingdom in different time frames and seasons; some are past tense, some are present tense, and others are in the future. It is easy for us to get confused about whether He is talking to us about the present age or something in the future.

As a result, various theories and philosophies have surfaced in the body of Christ about the kingdom of God. Some of them are kingdom-now-or-later, kingdom-now-not-yet, dominion-now-or-never, and many others you might have heard. The kingdom-now group believes God's kingdom must be fully established in the here and now, and the dominion-now group thinks we are supposed take over and rule the entire earth. We believe the Word teaches that we should be establishing the kingdom of God and see His will manifest in every spheres of influence, making head-way until Christ returns.

Unfortunately, there is another camp: I call them the 'I don't care-ever-camp'. These do not believe they should have any involvement in the world around them at all. Because of this rapture mentality, they have been in a holding pattern, waiting and waiting, and have succumbed to a "don't touch, don't care" attitude.

They tend to think that anything that happens on the earth and in our nations doesn't matter, because we are going to be *outta here any minute*, so why care? However, there is very little scriptural support for this belief. As students of the Word, it is imperative for us to understand what pertains to us and what is waiting to be revealed in the future.

Another misconception we have had was that because the church is in existence, we are restraining evil from manifesting in our nations, or restraining evil from overtaking our cities and neighborhoods. Take the United States as an example: What evil was the church able to restrain in America over the last seventy years?

When abortion was legalized, the church couldn't do anything about it. As a result, more than three million children have been murdered. Prayer was taken out of our schools with disastrous results for our children and the education system as a whole. Now, they've started using same-sex teaching materials to elementary school children, as part of sex education for children under ten years old. With the legalization of same-sex marriage, our government has redefined the most valuable foundation of our life and faith, one that is very close to our heart: marriage and family. The coming decades will show the results of that decision all too clearly.

Now they are trying to eliminate gender difference altogether and leaving this "choice" to the children themselves. Today a child is expected to "decide" which gender they want to be when they grow up! The tragedy of 9/11 took thousands of innocent lives. Marijuana has been legalized, and now there is talk about legalizing pedophilia. Next would be incest and bestiality. What influence has the church had in restraining any of these menaces from manifesting in our culture? Very little. All the while, Christians claim to be the majority of the American population and claimed to have had more revivals than any other country in the modern day.

All of this is happening because we have been brain washed about our assignment on earth. The most important message Jesus preached was about the coming of His kingdom to earth, bringing heaven to earth. The most popular message preached today is taking people to heaven. Something has gone drastically wrong.

The kingdom of God has been revealed to us in the Bible in seven different dimensions and operations. Unless we get a clear understanding of that, we will be ineffective. We will only be able to talk the talk, and will not be able to walk the walk.

When we read the Gospels we need to keep these seven dimensions and operations of the kingdom of God in mind. Many readers get confused when they read what Jesus said in the Gospels about the kingdom of God. Because of that, they throw the baby out with the bathwater and totally reject the teaching of the kingdom of God, in spite of the fact that it is the most important subject in the New Testament. I grew up in church for twenty-five years and never once heard a sermon on the kingdom of God.

I spent five years of life in seminary, there was not a single teaching or subject on the kingdom of God. It is really sad.

Many well-intentioned people look at me with suspicion when I talk about the kingdom. The kingdom message has been hidden from them; and for some unknown reason, they believe that if anyone talks or preaches about the kingdom, they are in error. This happens because of the deception of the enemy.

The Holy Spirit's intention through this book is to clear up that confusion from the hearts of believers, so they can have the knowledge of the truth that sets them free, and receive everything God has for them right now. My goal is that the church can become everything God intended her to be. Let me tell you something emphatically: *Without the teaching and revelation of the kingdom of God, the church will not become everything God intended her to be.* It is impossible, no matter how many revivals we may have, what kind of music we play, and how large our building or congregation is.

Trying to build a church without the kingdom is like constructing a building without a foundation, or a nation without a government. It's just a matter of time before everything comes crashing down and all of our efforts are wasted. This has happened throughout the centuries and that is why great churches disappear or dwindle over time. The kingdom of God is the foundation of not just our life here on earth, but the universe itself. The entire universe exists as part of His kingdom and for His kingdom.

If we do not understand the kingdom of God, we will not understand our purpose and what God has been trying to accomplish on the earth. Nor will we understand our responsibility toward our society and how to respond when evil manifests. We blame end-time philosophies or the devil, and have been doing that for generations.

When most people hear the kingdom message, they immediately think of something futuristic, meaning something Jesus will set up on the earth after His second coming. Or they may think of the kingdom Jesus talked about while He was on earth. They are not taught much about the eternal kingdom or the present kingdom that is operating on the earth right now.

What do I mean by seven dimensions and operations of the kingdom? God has revealed and manifested His kingdom in seven different ways throughout Scripture. The kingdom did not manifest the same way every time in every age. Depending on man's cooperation and participation, God allowed what we could handle.

For example, in the Gospels we read different verses about the kingdom, which seem confusing to people. At first, Jesus said the kingdom of God had not yet arrived (Matthew 4:17). He came to announce the imminent arrival of it by saying it was at hand, or very near. That doesn't mean it was not in existence. It existed, but in a different realm. That is what I mean by different dimensions.

Next, Jesus said the kingdom of God is within us (Luke 17:21). How did something that was near appear within us? Then He said, "And He said to them, "Assuredly, I say to you that there are some standing here who will not taste death till they see the kingdom of God present with power." (Mark 9:1). Jesus makes similar statements in Matthew 16:28 and in Luke 9:27. How something that is already within us, going to appear in the future? He was talking about three different dimensions and operations of the kingdom in different time frames.

Each time you come across the mention of the kingdom in the Bible, you need to decipher it so you can understand the time frame in which that dimension of the kingdom would manifest. If we don't do that, we will misinterpret the Word and end up in error. Every reference to the kingdom of God in the Gospels is not meant for this day and age. Some of them are meant for us now, and others for the age to come. In Luke 22:30 Jesus said, "that you may eat and drink at My table in My kingdom, and sit on thrones judging the twelve tribes of Israel." This is for the future. He also said this: "And I say to you that many will come from east and west, and sit down with Abraham, Isaac, and Jacob in the kingdom of heaven" (Matthew 8:11).

Though God is the Creator of time, He lives outside of time. Any Scripture in the Bible can be lived in any age, time, and place. God has not put any time limit on any of His Word, only a faith limit. *If you can believe it, you can appropriate it.*

If you read the hall of fame of faith in Hebrews 11, you will see that all of those people lived by faith and obtained righteousness from God. Anyone could have done it; there were no exceptions or favorites. Each was highlighted because of their faith.

That is why Jesus said that Abraham wished to see and live in one of His days and He did it by faith (John 8:56). David lived in the age of grace by faith. You may ask, what about the prophecies in Isaiah that say, "The nursing child shall play by the cobra's hole, and the weaned child shall put his hand in the viper's den" (Isaiah 11:8)? Can we live out that prophecy practically now? Yes, of course. There is much evidence in the Bible and modern day in which people lived with wild animals as friends and they did not harm them.

Daniel in the lion's den is the best example. Perhaps Daniel used one of those lions as his pillow at night! He did not sit in the corner of the den crouched in fear all night long. If he did, it was Daniel's problem and not God's. He could have easily used a lion as his pillow. I have read many accounts of people in the church age who encountered wild animals in their travels and were not harmed. Instead the animals behaved in a friendly manner and helped them in many ways. You can research online to find more about this. You don't need to be saved to have this experience. Many unsaved people are living with wild animals.

I believe and pray God will use this book to clear up every misconception and misunderstanding we have about the kingdom of God. Unless we are clear on this, we cannot move forward, and will waver back and forth without doctrinal stability. May the Lord use this book to accomplish this goal.

Abraham John

Introduction

The church is still the solution for every problem we face. Believers are supposed to be on the forefront of innovation, leadership, and research and development in every nation because the most creative Person lives inside of us.

The church is supposed to be the solution for all of the problems the world is facing because we represent God and His kingdom to the earth and its inhabitants. The church is the only visible manifestation of the invisible kingdom of God. Humans are the only visible manifestation of an invisible God. *That means those who see the church should see the kingdom of God, and those who see us should know what God is like.* If not, we have failed in our mission.

If we only sing and have a twenty-minute teaching on a Sunday morning, we are telling the people out there that God is all about singing and giving a pithy sermon. How much are we forfeiting and fooling the people instead of doing what we were originally created to do?

If there is an economic problem in a nation, the church should have the solution because Jesus became poor to deliver us from the curse of poverty. We are supposed to be witnessing what Jesus accomplished through His life and death on the cross to the world (2 Corinthians 8:9).

If there is a social or racial problem on earth, the church should have the solution to that problem because God has given us the ministry and the word of reconciliation (2 Corinthians 5:18).

If there is a health problem in any nation, the church should have the solution to that problem because Jesus died and paid for our sickness, and by His stripes we are healed (1 Peter 2:24; Revelations 22:2).

If there is violence or hopelessness in our cities and streets, the church should have the solution to that problem because Jesus is our peace and hope (Romans 15:13; Ephesians 2:14).

If there is a hunger problem in any nation, the church should have the solution to that problem because Jesus told His disciples to feed the multitudes (Mark 6:37).

If there are people dying on the streets without food and clothing, the church should have the solution to that problem. Jesus said that if we do that we will inherit the eternal kingdom of God (Matthew 25:34-36).

If there are marriage or family problems, the church should have the solutions to those problems because God instituted the first family on earth (Matthew 19:3-6).

If there is a human trafficking or child abuse problem, the church should have the solution to that problem. Righteousness and justice are the foundation of His throne (Psalm 89:14).

If there is purposelessness in the lives of people, the church should have their solution. The Bible is the only book that reveals the purpose of mankind (Genesis 1:26).

If there are political problems or problems in government the church should have the solution. The government is supposed to be upon Jesus' shoulders. Governmental authority came from God, and the constitutions in most countries were taken from values and moral standards revealed in the Bible (Isaiah 9:6; Romans 13:1).

INTRODUCTION

If there is a gender identity crisis in our nation, the church should have the solution to that problem. The Bible talks about gender identity and the responsibilities of each gender (Genesis 1:27).

If all authority and the keys of God's kingdom have been given to the church, and the entire jurisdiction of the earth has been delivered to the church based on Matthew 16:19, then who is responsible for what is happening on the earth right now? Whom did God hold responsible for what happened in the garden in the beginning? Adam, right?

The moment the church recognizes her role and accepts responsibility for what is happening in the nations, the turnaround will begin. Instead, we have developed a we-don't-belong-here mentality. This mindset was instilled in us by the religious spirit so we will avoid what is happening in our nations instead of confronting it.

What if people like Joseph, Abraham, Moses, Esther, Daniel, and Paul had lived with an "I-don't-belong-here" attitude? This world would be in worse shape than we see today. Jesus did not give the keys of His kingdom to a government or political leader, but to the church. Sadly, we have been using those keys to "bind" the wrong thing for almost two thousand years. And we have been "loosing" cohorts of demonic forces to the earth unknowingly through the negative words we speak. Each time we speak a negative word we are empowering, releasing, and activating demons to operate on the earth. This should not be!

Do you think we will solve these problems if we meet on a Sunday morning for an hour and a half? How do we expect the world to change? Many people are tired of the established church. They are jumping out of it as people do from a sinking ship, regardless of which denomination they belong. Our churches are filled with people who are fifty years or older, and most of them are just hanging in there, waiting for the rapture to happen.

It will take an entirely different style, system, and method of training if we really expect to make a serious impact for God on this earth. There is nothing God is withholding from us. He made everything on earth and in heaven at our disposal. The only thing we lack is the proper understanding and the systems to steward His wealth and various resources.

Over time, the church became more concerned about what is happening in heaven and who lives there, than about the planet God entrusted us to take care of. He will not hold us responsible for heaven or for something we did not do in heaven, but He will surely hold us responsible for what we do and do not do to this earth while we are here.

Please read Jesus' last parable before He went to the cross (Luke 19:11-27). There are many books about heaven and what is happening there, but not many about what we are supposed to do with the earth. More than ninety-eight percent of the Bible is about our life here and how people lived out their purpose for God and His kingdom. I have not found a single reference in the Bible about any human doing anything in heaven for God except the twenty-four elders mentioned in Revelation.

The religious spirit has brainwashed the church for hundreds of years and made us believe that heaven belongs to us and we were created to live there and sing for all eternity. *It's not in the Bible.*

The church has been training people to live in heaven when it is supposed to train people to reign on earth. That's one of its purposes. If we are going to train our children to reign, we need to begin when they are very young. We should not let our children's minds be programmed by the ways of Babylon.

What are the ways of Babylon? Individualism, personal success, movies, sports, fun, and religion are some of the ways of Babylon. Every parent dreams that his or her child will grow up to be a superstar because we are living in a culture that idolizes movie and sports stars. We spend the first fifteen years training our children to become like them, but we do not invest time teaching them the ways of God. This is tragic. Our focus is on the wrong things. We no longer teach our children what it means to

INTRODUCTION

be a man or a woman, or why God created humans either. Why? We don't have the time or the materials to train them. So, as a result, many became depressed and disillusioned and end up committing suicide because they couldn't become a super star.

The Lord put in my heart to prepare books that teach children from birth and up about their Purpose, Identity, and Source. Those are the three age-old questions every individual asks: "Who am I? Where did I come from? Why am I here?" Unless each individual can answer those questions with confidence, their life will not go well.

That is why Jesus came as a human being: to show us the will of the Father concerning our lives. The first human messed up and so has everyone after him. Therefore, God sent another Human to show us what He expects from each of us. Jesus came to show us how to live and fulfill our purpose.

Did Jesus spend His time on earth singing to His Father? How many references do you see in the Gospels to that? Did He teach His disciples about choir techniques? Did He conduct special worship nights in the temple with smoke machines and special sound effects from heaven? Did He cry to be with His Father in heaven because life on earth was too hard for Him? No. He did none of that.

Jesus said He glorified His Father by finishing the works He gave Him to do (John 17:4). Will we all be able to say that with confidence at the end of our lives? Paul said it. He said that he finished his course and completed the race that God had set before him (2 Timothy 4:7).

Many are confused about what the Father expects from them. They complete different religious exercises, thinking it will make Him happy. Others try to go back to Jewish roots, thinking that is what He expects from them.

Jesus said that we are the salt of the earth and light of this world. Many believers act as if Jesus said they are the salt and light of heaven.

There is no need of any salt and light in heaven. If you prepare a meal and add no salt to it, you can imagine how it will taste. It won't have any flavor. Life on this earth is becoming tasteless. Why? Because the salt is not functioning as it should.

Jesus said that if the salt loses its savor, what good is it except to be thrown to the ground and trampled? (Matthew 5:13). That is what is happening to the church in many parts of the world. They are being thrown to the ground and trampled.

Jesus also said that we do not light a candle and put it under a basket, but instead we should put it on a lampstand so it can give light to people who are in darkness (Matthew 5:15). There are many today who are living in darkness because the light is not shining.

God is raising up an army of people from every nation. These are not the usual believers who *go to* church on a Sunday morning. These *are* the church, *the ekklesia* of God who are beginning to function as the church should function, seven days a week in their community and workplace. God is doing a new thing on this planet and this Kingdom Awareness Series is meant for those precious people.

Chapter 1
Sevenfold Transition

Chapter - 1

Sevenfold Transition

How many of you remember the fear and anticipation just before Y2K? Many believers filled their basements with water and emergency supplies in case something went wrong. The whole world was in the grip of the unknown. Was this the end of the world? Was the rapture imminent? Others said the Antichrist would appear and great tribulation would soon begin. As you know now, it was all nonsense.

Eighteen years later we are still here, and none of those things the experts in the religious and political world warned would happen came to pass. There are people out there who are promoting emergency food supplies and survival equipment on Christian television and making money. There is nothing wrong to be prepared for an emergency.

I was at a conference in the year 2000, and a well-known prophet was one of the speakers. He said he was going to announce a word that the Lord wanted him to release to the body of Christ. Great anticipation gripped everyone. Some expected him to announce when the rapture was going to happen, or that another big revival was going to hit their town.

During the last meeting of the last day of the conference the prophet said he was going to release the word. People practically held their breath in rapt attention, and finally he blurted out something nobody expected: "By the year 2000, the church age has officially came to an end. We are now entering the kingdom age."

Everybody was in shock, mouths hanging open. That wasn't the word we were expecting. Nobody knew what to do with it. They did not receive it, so most did nothing and went back to life as usual, continuing with what they always did and somehow expecting a different result.

They did not know what was expected of them or what to do differently in a kingdom age. Nobody started educating them because they didn't take the word seriously. They were brought up in the church age. They all believed the church age would end with the rapture of the church. Nobody taught them about the kingdom or what a kingdom age looks like.

Every age requires a different mindset and subsequent set of actions. Right now the church is coming to a very early stage of understanding what the kingdom age looks like and what we are supposed to do with it.

God's kingdom is not limited to time or space. It's an everlasting kingdom and His dominion endures for all generations (Psalm 145:13). The *operating system* and the *vehicle* He uses to establish it and His will on earth varies from age to age. The equation goes something like this:

The Age – Kingdom - Operating System - the Vehicle - Manifestation

Age	Kingdom/ OS	Vehicle/Manifestation
Old Testament	Law	Nation of Israel
New Testament	Grace	Church

In the Old Testament the operating system God used to establish the kingdom was the Mosaic Law. He told them He wanted them to be "a kingdom of priests and a holy nation" (Exodus 19:6). The vehicle He worked through was the people or the nation of Israel. The manifestation of His work among them was that the nation of Israel became the most blessed nation on earth. They were the head, above every other nation.

In the New Testament the operating system is grace and the vehicle is the church. His purpose remains the same throughout all ages, but the system and the vehicle varies. We are called a kingdom of priests and a holy nation as well (1 Peter 2:9). We haven't seen the full manifestation of the kingdom of God yet because we have been waiting to escape. The whole creation is groaning and waiting, not for our escape but for our manifestation (Romans 8:19-22).

After that word, more prophecies began to emerge saying the body of Christ was in a transition. I also prophesied it many times. I did not know what we were transitioning into. At that time nobody knew, so we kept on repeating the same thing, and kept doing what we always did.

Transition means we are in-between something. When I fly overseas, there is usually a layover somewhere, depending on where I am going. If I travel to Africa, there will be a layover somewhere in Europe. If I am traveling to South Africa and my layover is in London or in Dubai, those places are not my final destination. I am just there temporarily for a few hours till I jump onto my next flight.

While I am waiting at those airports, I am in transition. That is the best way I can explain the word *transition*. You are in-between something. The body of Christ has been in that position since the year 2000. Some say we are heading into another revival or the greatest revival, and others say we are on the verge of an imminent rapture. Is that what God is really up to, or is He doing something totally different than we are expecting? After all, His thoughts and ways are higher than ours.

Only recently the Holy Spirit gave me insight about what we are transitioning into. He said the transition is happening in seven different levels, and with seven being the perfect number and also the number of God, I figured that God was speaking this to me.

In the next pages I will reveal the seven different levels of transition that we have been in. We have not arrived at our final destination yet. We are still in the layover period. Anytime a season or age changes, though it happens in a moment of time, there is always a long process involved for the change to be completed.

When the age of grace began with the birth of Jesus, not everyone opened their arms to receive Him and the grace He was ushering in. God sent His messengers to announce the arrival of the new, but most religious people stayed put and were not willing to change. The religious world continued to sell animals and birds for offering sacrifices while God moved on with His agenda. Could something similar be happening right now? Have we for so long been trying to resurrect what God wanted put to rest?

Another example is when Jesus left the temple in Jerusalem in Matthew 24, which was the beginning of a new era. God was leaving a physical temple system made of bricks and mortar, for a temple that He always wanted, which is us; humans. Jesus will never again enter a temple that is a physical building. But the religious leaders continued to venerate a building because it benefitted them financially.

Every time something new happens in any field, there are people who are open to change, and there are others who stick with what they already know. We see this in technology, science, fashion, and the list goes on. It's not common to see someone who still uses an old flip-phone when smart phones are so much more useful. Though many can afford to upgrade, they refuse to change because change requires a new mindset, and a new mindset requires learning some new methods and techniques, which they don't like.

Why is there a growing dissatisfaction among believers toward the current church? There are more believers in the U.S. who do not attend any church than those who go to a church on a Sunday morning. Those numbers increase weekly. Believers sense in their spirit that there is something missing. They are thinking that there has to be more than what they are experiencing in their places of worship. Many do not know how to articulate that, but that is what is in their hearts.

Meanwhile, leaders are not willing to change anything because they are afraid that if they change what they have been doing for decades, will they lose members and offering money. They know that what they are doing is not working and not bringing the same result as it did when they began; but they fail to recognize that the season has changed and God has moved on to something new.

Smart leaders will catch hold of what God is doing and make the necessary changes before their ship sinks. I would like to share what the Holy Spirit has put in my heart about what He is doing right now in the church. As with any new season in any aspect of life, people who were smart adapted to the change quickly and utilized the opportunity. May the Lord give grace and wisdom to our leaders to make the necessary changes before it's too late.

Seven Levels of Transition

1. From the Church Age to a Kingdom Age

I will start with what that prophet said eighteen years ago. I did not understand what he meant at that time. I do now in part. Everywhere I go I hear people talking about the kingdom more than ever. That is really encouraging. *Kingdom* has become the buzz word of the day.

Life on earth began with the kingdom in the garden of Eden. It will end or transition when "the kingdoms of this world" become "the kingdoms of our Lord and of His Christ" as it says in Revelation 11:15. We lost the kingdom with the fall; and ever since then, God has been trying to restore it to mankind and the earth. Jesus began His ministry with the preaching of the kingdom and ended His ministry with the same. The church age began with the preaching of the kingdom, and Jesus said it will end with the preaching of it too (Matthew 24:14).

God's plan from the beginning of time has been to establish His kingdom and His will on earth as it is in heaven. His plans have been delayed and deviated because of the rebellion of mankind. He will not change His mind about it nor change His plan for the earth and mankind. His counsel will stand forever and ever.

As I say in most of my books, the entire Bible is about a King, His kingdom, His government, His royal family, and His plan for the planet Earth. That's the Bible in a nutshell. If we do not look at the Bible and life on earth from that perspective, we will not be in alignment with what God is doing. We will be off track.

We have been so focused on the church (a building) that we missed the kingdom. God doesn't want the whole planet to be turned into a mega church, as many churches have become today. Nor does He want to see us all in heaven. He will not get anything out of that scenario. There is not a single verse in the Bible that says humans are doing anything in heaven. That itself should shake every religious bone in us! God wants the whole planet to be turned into His kingdom. He wants His will to be accomplished here as it is in heaven.

In the Bible, every person who had a revelation of heaven saw the throne of God (Isaiah 6:1; Daniel 7:9). Remember: Heaven is His throne (Isaiah 66:1). They did not see pets and flowers, like some of the modern revelations from people who claim they visited heaven. When Paul was caught up into the third heaven he said he heard words that are not lawful for him to speak. Why it is illegal for an apostle to speak on earth the language or sounds he heard in heaven? Why didn't he see flowers and pets instead?

As mentioned earlier, many believe and preach that the church is restraining or holding back evil from manifesting. Let me ask you an honest question. How much has church been able to do that in the last seventy years? What evil was the church able to restrain from manifesting in the USA? When Roe versus Wade took place and changed our laws, the church was not able to stop it. All that's been done since has not been able to turn it back.

When prayer was taken out of schools, we mourned it but have never been able to change that either. Marriage and family, the most spiritual and foundational institution of our existence was redefined through the American courts and now homosexual and lesbian marriages have been legalized. On 9/11 terrorists attacked, and America went to war. That situation has not improved. Now abortion is legal, prayer is only allowed if initiated by a student, gender differences are being removed, and Americans live in fear — while the church goes in and does another musical production on Sunday morning, thinking it might help their nation.

No matter where you live, examine whether or not the church has been able to restrain evil. How is your area doing in that? According to Jesus, if the gates of hell are prevailing against His church in a city, then that church is not fulfilling its purpose. It lost its saltiness.

When we fully move into the kingdom age, our focus becomes establishing God's kingdom and will on earth, instead of trying to take people to heaven. God doesn't want humans up in heaven doing anything for Him. He wants us down here on earth doing what He always wanted us to do. *Are we anywhere close to achieving that goal?*

I leave that to you to answer for yourself. Just look around and you will understand what I am talking about. We have a long way to go. The church has been doing everything except what Jesus commanded. What did He really command us to do? That bring us to the next level of transition.

2. From Evangelizing the World to Discipling Nations

Somewhere along the line, someone came up with the idea that the Great Commission was all about evangelism, but Jesus didn't even mention evangelism in the Great Commission in Matthew 28. If you do not believe me, read the verses below.

> And Jesus came and spoke to them, saying, "All authority has been given to Me in heaven and on earth. Go therefore and make disciples of all the nations, baptizing them in the name of the Father and of the Son and of the Holy Spirit, teaching them to observe all things that I have commanded you; and lo, I am with you always, even to the end of the age." Amen (Matthew 28:18-20).

For a long time, I understood these verses as if Jesus said, "Go therefore and evangelize and make disciples *from* all nations." I thought it was an individual mandate, but Jesus did not give an individual mandate. He gave a national mandate: discipling nations. He did not say *from* all nations, but *of* all nations. In Greek it actually means, "Having gone therefore disciple all the nations." We are supposed to disciple nations. How do we do that? Is that even possible in our day and age?

Do you see the word *evangelism* anywhere in the above verses? Did He say, "Go and evangelize the world?" I don't see it. Before the year 2000, I heard about mega-evangelism programs by many large organizations like the AD2000 Movement and the 10/40 Window movements. Just as we turned the word *worship* into singing, we switched *discipling* nations into *evangelizing* them.

We interpreted these verses as "go and evangelize the world." We thought Jesus was telling us to go and win souls. I can tell you from my experience that *Jesus means what He says, and He says what He means.* He won't say one thing and mean something different (as most humans do). How could we miss what He had stated so plain and simply? Just like we missed everything else! We missed it through the deception of the religious spirit.

Jesus said to go and make disciples of all nations. He talked about discipling nations, and we have been training and helping people on how to evangelize instead: two different jobs that create two entirely different results in the end. If our evangelism and winning souls are geared toward discipling nations, then it's good; but if our only intention is taking people to heaven, then we missed the target.

We evangelized the world and as a result, we have brought many souls into the kingdom, but we have lost all the nations. Jesus wanted nations, not just souls. He is the King of all nations, and they are His inheritance (Psalm 2:7-8). When He comes back He wants nations serving Him, not just souls or individuals waiting to fly out of here.

That means we are entering into a season of discipling nations. I don't mean there won't be any more evangelism. That will continue until Jesus comes back, but those who have been evangelized already and have been waiting to fly away in the rapture need to engage in discipling their cities and nations. It has begun in many nations. God is raising up His people to take their places in government, media, and every other place of influence. Thank You, Jesus! Finally, the body of Christ is grasping the heart and plan of God.

When we disciple a nation, what will the end result look like? The entire nation — from the president or prime minister to the cobbler down the street — will be serving God and working toward establishing His kingdom and will in that nation.

The church has failed terribly in teaching believers what happens to them when they are born again. The main focus became getting *fire insurance* to escape hell and go to heaven. Nobody "sold" salvation like that in the Bible. According to Jesus, when we are born again we only "see" the kingdom (John 3:3). We have whole churches of believers in which the majority of them are just surviving till the rapture happens.

It should never have been that way. We do not have the right programs to train believers how to become the light of *this world* and salt of *this earth*. We have been waiting to become a light in heaven, but there is no need of light in heaven.

Heaven is not in any need of our help. The only place we can do something for God or establish the kingdom is here on the earth. That's why God put us here in the first place. Once people come into the kingdom, the next stage should be to equip them and release them to disciple their nation. Everybody can do something in that process.

To disciple a nation we need to know what comprises that nation. I had great zeal for winning souls. Anytime I could not share the gospel with someone I felt guilty and bad. I thought it was my responsibility to save souls; if I did not do it, then God would hold me responsible for their blood.

I believed and felt this way for many years. Then one day the Holy Spirit revealed to me why Jesus and the apostles were not running around trying to save everyone they saw. They were very strategic in their mission. Jesus was not running all throughout Israel trying to save everyone. That really shocked me and also answered many questions I carried in my heart. Jesus was very relaxed and did not condemn the people for not believing in Him; He only confronted the religious leaders. Paul selected very strategic and metropolitan cities of his time to establish churches. There is a specific reason behind this too.

I had to rid the religious spirit out of my life. When that happened, I saw my life and the world around me through God's perspective for the first time. This was the most life-changing experience in my life.

I now understood that God wants nations to serve Him, not just souls. The saved believers in a nation should be focusing on how to disciple their nation and bring it under the headship of Jesus Christ our King, instead of waiting for the rapture or tribulation to happen.

The Son is waiting for one thing. The Father told Him to sit at His right hand, until He makes His enemies His footstool (Hebrews 10:12-13).

3. From Going around the World to Going into the World

Another thing Jesus said that we have misunderstood is found in Mark 16:

> And He said to them, "Go *into* all the world and preach the gospel to *every creature*" (Mark 16:15).

We thought He said, "Go *around* the whole world (travel to different countries) and preach the gospel to every human." That is not what He said. He said to *go into* the world. There is a big difference. For a long time, our perspective has been that this world is not our home and that we should stay away from it as much as we can, but we cannot live on the earth without being *in* the world.

Jesus was giving us the clue to disciple on how to disciple nations. To disciple a nation we need to go into the world system. The Greek used for world is *kosmos* which means the orderly system by which the universe operates. The world includes everything.

Earth is the physical planet, and the world is the system by which the earth functions. There is no world without the earth and there will be nothing on the earth without the world. The world keeps the earth productive and fruitful.

The sad part is that the devil took over the world and established himself as the god of it. He knew that if he could control the world he could keep the earth to himself. And that is what he did. Then, he used the world system to establish his kingdom here so he could accomplish his will through it.

Originally the earth and the world belonged to God. He created them both.

> He was in the world, and the world was made through Him, and the world did not know Him (John 1:10).

> The earth is the Lord's, and all its fullness, the world and those who dwell therein (Psalm 24:1).

God has been in the process of redeeming this world. He paid the price and gave the rest for us to do. We are the ones who messed up the earth and gave the world over to the devil. Ever since that time, we have been in denial and have been waiting to escape this world. We have been taught that this world does not belong to us, but to the devil.

We have inherited a host of wrong beliefs and bad teachings. Very few people are willing to question where and who gave them to us. The first wrong concept we have is this one: This world does not belong to us.

We have been singing, "This world is not my home…" and "Oh take the whole world, but give me Jesus…" As a result the devil took the whole world from us and has been using it for his purposes and no one is questioning him.

The second one goes with it and says that since we are not of this world, we should not do anything in this world. Instead, we should wait until we get to heaven to fulfill our purpose.

The third wrong belief we have inherited is the idea that we should be separated from the world or its people. We called this idea *holiness*. If we view people in this light, Jesus, the apostles and all the saints in the Old Testament were not holy, because they were sent into the world and were not separate from its people. They did not just go around the world (Mark 16:15; John 17:18).

The fourth wrong belief we inherited is that this world is not our home. We've written many songs about this, and have been singing them for hundreds of years. It is as if we were like fish in the ocean, saying, "This water is not my home. I am going to wait to get to heaven to swim and live my life." How stupid is that? What if a bird woke up every morning and sang, "This forest is not my home. I am waiting to fly away into a forestless country so I can fly, sing, and live forever?" The rest of the creatures would say that bird had lost its mind.

If Christ created this world, and I am a coheir with Him, then this world is part of my inheritance. That is what the apostle Paul taught the early church.

> Therefore let no one boast in men. For all things are yours: whether Paul or Apollos or Cephas, or the world or life or death, or things present or things to come—all are yours. And you are Christ's, and Christ is God's (1 Corinthians 3:21-23).

Thank God he did not tell them to wait until they could fly away!

Abraham, the father of our faith, was called an heir of the world (Romans 4:13).

The above verses say everything belongs to us. The main thing that is keeping us away from our inheritance is a faulty belief system taught by the religious spirit. My personal testimony is almost the same. According to my culture, the youngest son in the family will inherit the family's house and care for the parents. I am the youngest son in my family.

Technically, the family (my parent's) house should have been mine. Because I did not understand my father and had a wrong concept about his love for me, I denied my inheritance and did not appreciate what he wanted to give me. I told my father to give it to my elder brother, which he did. Who was the loser in the end? Me.

This is what has happened to many believers. We have a wrong understanding about our Father, His love for us, and why He put us all here in the first place. We do not appreciate what He created and gave to us to manage. We have been in denial and have given everything to the devil. The Lord asked me a few weeks ago, "How does the earth benefit from us being here? What good have we done to it?"

Think about it. We have been using its resources for thousands of years and living by it. I do not think we appreciate the Lord for what He created and for sustaining us this long. Just think about that for a minute. God raises up some non-religious people who have the burden to fix things that are broken on the earth and He blesses them with the wisdom and resources to do it.

We complain to our children that we deserve respect and gratitude because we have been taking care of them for a few years and have brought them up. How much longer has the earth been sustaining us and providing for us with everything we need since before we were even born? What have we been doing for it in return? Each day we keep destroying it little by little, and layer by layer.

When Jesus comes back, the Bible says He will destroy those who destroyed the earth (Revelation 11:18). That's should be a startling revelation. That verse should be posted on the front door of every church.

The question is: How do we redeem the world? That is why Jesus said to go *into* the world and preach the gospel to *every creature*. We need to go into the systems of this world and demonstrate the gospel of the kingdom by healing, fixing, and restoring what is broken. That is why He also said to preach the gospel to all creatures, not just humans. In Colossians 1:23, Paul said he preached the gospel to every creature under heaven.

This world has been already judged, and the ruler of it has already been cast out (John 12:31; 16:8-11). Whatever the enemy has been doing, he is doing it illegally because no one is enforcing the judgment that Jesus pronounced over him.

Every creature was affected by the fall of man, and they need to be redeemed. The blood of Jesus is powerful and sufficient to redeem and restore all the damage that the fall brought upon on our planet.

Everything that came under "corruption" or bondage because of the fall of man needs to hear the gospel of redemption. They came under bondage because of man. Now it's the responsibility of man to restore it. God did His part in Christ Jesus and gave the rest for us to do.

> For the earnest expectation of the creation eagerly waits for the revealing of the sons of God…because the creation itself also will be delivered from the bondage of corruption into the glorious liberty of the children of God. For we know that the whole creation groans and labors with birth pangs together until now (Romans 8:19, 21-22).

We did not know how to go into the world, neither did we know how to redeem creation because we have been staying away from it. We have not trained our people with the skills and capacity to do it. We do not know how the political system works and we do not know much about how the economy works either. The enemy took hold of those areas and put his people in key places to ensure that his will is done through those systems. This must change!

God is raising up a new breed of believers and has been equipping them to go *into* the world. He did not send His son to *end* the world, but to *save* it.

> For God did not send His Son into the world to condemn the world, but that the world through Him might be saved (John 3:17; 12:47).

It's time for the church and Jesus to have the same dream. All this time we have had a different dream than Jesus. Subsequently, we were working against His plans. He has been trying to save the world, and we have been waiting for the end of it. He has given us work to do and we have been focused on escape. Which one do you think will succeed in the end? Our dream or His?

The question is this: How do we go into the world? To begin with, we need to understand what the Bible means by the term "world." The world or *kosmos* (in Greek) means any orderly system here on earth. The world system is comprised of eight main ingredients: culture; religion; government; economy; education; media and entertainment; and science, technology, and nature. We need to go into each of these spheres and preach and demonstrate the gospel of the kingdom to restore it to God's original design. That is what every prophet has spoken since the world began.

> "Whom (Jesus) heaven must receive until the times of restoration of all things, which God has spoken by the mouth of all His holy prophets since the world began" (Acts 3:21).

How much have we restored so far?

Jesus said, "As You sent Me into the world, I also have sent them into the world" (John 17:18). He did not go around the world, but was sent into it. Then He sent us into the world.

We need new kinds of training centers and seminaries to equip believers to go into the world. As a ministry, we are preparing courses to start our online university to do the same. If you are interested in learning more about going into the world, please read the other volumes in the kingdom series.

4. From a Religious Church into a Kingdom *Ekklesia*

With the current system and the state in which the church operates, we have brought in the maximum number of people that the church can handle. That's why there are more people leaving the church than joining it. If more people need to be won to Christ, then we need a different operating system. That is what the kingdom *ekklesia* is all about.

Ekklesia is the word Jesus used when He spoke to His disciples about the church. It was a term with which they were very familiar, and originated in Greece where it referred to the ruling body of Athens which was called together by a herald. Jesus called us out to rule in a similar fashion.

What do secular people envision when they think of church? They see buildings with crosses on top on almost every street corner. They think that's the place where Christians come together to worship on Sunday. The church has become a religious symbol to the world, and a social center for Christians. God never intended for His church to be associated with any religion or a particular type of building. He planned for relationships, not buildings.

The church is supposed to be the political center of God's kingdom on earth. Ekklesia was a political term used in Greek culture, not for a building where people came once a week to sing and to hear someone preach.

When I travel across Europe, I see huge cathedrals that people call churches. Most of them are empty and remain tourist attractions. That's not the church for which Jesus died to establish. Many of them are being turned into mosques.

What was in Jesus' mind when He thought of establishing the church in the first place? What came to the disciples' mind when Jesus said the word *church* for the first time? Let's think about this from Jesus' perspective.

Even if there is a church on every street corner, nothing will change for the better. To be honest, if you travel to some states in America, you can actually see a church on every street corner. However, if you really dive into the life of that city or town, you can see that the gates of hell have been holding and prevailing in that city for many years without anyone challenging them.

You cannot have a kingdom *ekklesia* while the gates of hell operate right next door to it. It's impossible. It's either one or the other, not both. It's either Jesus or the devil. That is what happened in places where Paul traveled and ministered: either the idol worshippers or the kingdom of God prevailed. Only one was reigning at a time.

The church we have today does not look or operate anything like what Jesus was intending when He mentioned the church. The system we have today is the product of religion: one we have divided into various segments called denominations with everyone claiming that theirs is the true church. If every denomination is claiming they are the true church, that itself proves none of them are. *Christ is not divided.* Scripture says there is "one Lord, one faith, one baptism, one God and Father of all, who is above all, and through all, and in you all" (Ephesians 4:5-6). Jesus is Head of one body. He also said that He wants one flock under one Shepherd (John 10:16).

Jesus is a King, and He came with the kingdom message to give His kingdom back to us. I hope you have already read some of the other books in the Kingdom Awareness series published by this ministry. I have explained these concepts thoroughly in other books, but here it is briefly: Every kingdom needs a king, and every king needs a governing body (or *ekklesia*) to rule the kingdom and establish his will in the territories of his kingdom. That is what Jesus intended when He established the church as the governing body of His kingdom; it is supposed to administer His kingdom and establish His will.

That is the purpose of the church and that is what He meant when He said, "I will build My church (*ekklesia*), and the gates of Hades shall not prevail against it" (Matthew 16:18).

I mentioned earlier that there are more people leaving the church today than the new people coming in. Why do people lose interest in church? The leaders blame the people and the culture. The people blame the leadership of the church. Possibly the main reason why people leave the church today, is because they are not finding solutions for their problems there. The church has lost its relevancy. They see the same problems in the church that they see in the world. To make matters worse, most of the times they can find better help out in the world rather than in the church.

When was the last time an unsaved person came into the church looking for help because we did something better than what they could find elsewhere? When have they come looking for expertise in some area? Very rarely. People might come to church for free food or used clothes; meanwhile we constantly go to the world for products, solutions, and expertise. It should not be that way! We are the light of this world and salt of the earth, not the light of heaven and the salt of paradise. Light is the solution for darkness. We are supposed to be the head and above others in every community.

The church (or kingdom *ekklesia*) should have answers to every problem this world has. Hunger, social issues, racial problems, spiritual concerns, sickness, poverty, political strife, you name it: they should come to us to solve their problems. That's how we are supposed to function as the light of this world.

The mountain of the Lord should be higher and more glorious than any other mountains (Isaiah 2:2). Some people believe if we sing our songs a little louder and longer, God is going to come down and solve all the problems for us. He will not. It doesn't matter how long we sing. We are the body of Christ: that means we are the hands, feet, mouth, and mind of Christ. If we do not do something, God cannot do it either.

Believers in different places are beginning to receive a glimpse of this. Most of them are not part of an organized religious group. They are out there alone right now, but God will gather them from all corners of the earth. He is building a kingdom *ekklesia* in every nation on earth. It has only just begun.

Our God never does something twice the same way. If you look at many churches, they claim to not have a written liturgy for services, but in almost every service, we do the same things over and over again, just like any mainline denomination. Our programs are written in our minds. We claim we are led by the Holy Spirit and spiritually superior to others, but in truth, we are just like anyone else out there.

We haven't had a system update in the last five hundred years. All technology we use, and everything else in life has had many updates—except the program and the system we use in our churches. In my own lifetime, technology has gone through manifold updates and upgrades. The cassette tape I grew up using was replaced by CDs. Nowadays everyone is listening to music digitally instead of on CDs. The cellphone that we use today was not even in existence just twenty years ago.

The companies that hesitated to change with the times failed or faltered. Kodak and Nokia are a couple of examples of modern day companies. One of the reasons the church is losing membership is because we do not change with the time. We do not change with the season we are in or with what God is currently doing.

We still do what God did in previous generations, trying to copy that and expecting a different result now, but those old things are supposed to be completely wiped out. We do not have a problem adapting to new models and systems in other areas like cars, technology, and clothing, but we resist change when it comes to church. We are supposed to function like a kingdom or a nation would function. We have been operating as a religious organization for too long. That's the reason the world labeled us "religious" because of the repeated rituals we do every Sunday morning.

5. From Preaching the Gospel of Salvation to Preaching the Gospel of the Kingdom

When we think of salvation, we think of going to heaven. To my knowledge, no one thought that way in New Testament times. Jesus and the apostles never asked anyone if they wanted to go to heaven when they died. They never gave an altar call either. He also never sent anyone to preach the gospel of salvation. He sent them to preach the gospel of the kingdom, and He told us to do the same.

Jesus' own testimony was that He came to preach the gospel of the kingdom (Luke 4:43). The whole salvation plan came because of the fall of Adam. *Salvation* means to save us from everything the fall brought upon us and restore everything we lost in consequence of that sin. We did not lose heaven when Adam fell. We lost the kingdom and sovereignty over the earth.

We have been going around the world asking people to get saved without telling them what they are being saved from. Most people believe they are saved from hellfire, but that is only part of the story. Hellfire is the ultimate punishment for rejecting the salvation God offers through Jesus Christ. Nobody has taught them what they are saved from.

People are tired of their life and their problems. They are looking for solutions and they can't find any. Though they are "saved," their life is not different at all, so they are frustrated and angry at themselves and God.

This will only change when we accurately teach people what we lost because of the fall and what God wants to restore to them through salvation. To know more about the process of salvation, and the things we lost with the fall that were redeemed through Jesus, please read my book *Kingdom Secrets to Restoring Nations Back to God*.

6. From All Other Types of Evangelism to Kingdom Evangelism

You may have heard of power evangelism; prophetic and healing evangelism; prayer evangelism; and personal and crusade evangelism. As a result of all those types of evangelism, we have brought the souls we now have into the kingdom. Yet more than half of the world still has not been reached. If the rest of the people in the world need to come into the kingdom, then we need to use kingdom evangelism.

What is kingdom evangelism? Kingdom evangelism is witnessing Jesus as the King, Creator, Judge, and Lord of all the earth and nations. We have been witnessing Jesus as the Healer, Prophet, Shepherd, Teacher, and more, but we have neglected the other facets of who Christ is.

The ultimate purpose of the fivefold ministry gifts is to equip the body of Christ to manifest the fullness of Christ or come into the fullness of Christ. We have been operating for too long in a partial revelation of Christ (Ephesians 4:13).

I was listening to the history of foreign missionaries who went to India in the eighteenth and nineteenth century. They sacrificed their lives to change and laid the foundation for the creation of modern India. They created scripts for many languages, and even wrote dictionaries and grammar for those languages. They worked against social and cultural ills and injustice. They did not go there to take some people to heaven. Their goal was cultural and social transformation. They went *into* the world.

They built the best schools, started newspapers, and established hospitals and universities. Compare that with modern missionaries and evangelists. Today we compete to show how many people attended our crusades, who had the better musical production or choir, and who had the most comfortable seating. What problems do we solve for the nation and for the people? Almost none. No wonder people don't like the church and Christians anymore!

Consider missionaries like William Carey (the father of modern missions), Amy Carmichael, Hudson Taylor, and Mother Theresa. When they sent their mission reports to their home base, they did not report the size of the crowd in the crusades. That was not their focus in ministry.

Instead they had a longer lasting legacy and greater impact than all of the crusade-conducting evangelists in our time combined.

As I mentioned before, Jesus did not tell us to go and evangelize the world. He told us to go and make disciples of all nations. We have lost our mission, succumbed to the deception of the enemy, and became a religious group instead.

7. From the Wilderness to the Promised Land

God did not call us out for us to die in the wilderness. The church has been operating in the same wilderness mindset the Israelites had when they came out of Egypt. The whole purpose of the wilderness experience is to get Egypt and its ways out of us; to prepare us to reach the place where we live out our calling. The wilderness is never supposed to be a permanent place, but a place of transition to our Promised Land.

In the wilderness, we walk by feelings and emotions based on what we *see* God doing. We are commanded to walk by faith and not by sight. It is also a place where God miraculously provides for us and our life depends on miracles. The whole church world has been operating in that mode for too long.

It is also a place of just enough; we can't plant or build anything in the wilderness. It is to be a short-term journey until we reach the Promised Land. There is no productivity in the wilderness; it is a place of survival. The Israelites depended on Moses to hear from God for them and he was their hero in that and every other respect.

Sadly, the majority of the people in the Old and New Testament never finished their wilderness journey. For a New Testament believer, the Promised Land is where we begin to function and live out our destiny. When the people of Israel reached the Promised Land, the miraculous provision of manna ceased and the cloud by day and fire by night disappeared.

In the wilderness God does everything for us. In the Promised Land we need to learn to partner with God to produce what we need. We need to manufacture, farm, and build in order to fulfill our destiny. Jesus has been waiting a very long time for the church to finish her wilderness experience and enter her Promised Land. That's where the church will show forth her glory to the rest of the world.

We should be the most productive people on earth, but now, the church is the most consuming agency. We need to become the best farmers, innovators, politicians, teachers, doctors, lawyers, and business people in every nation. We should not be known just for our singing and charity works. We should be known for every good work. This will happen only when we complete our wilderness journey and enter our Promised Land.

We cannot enter and function in the Promised Land with a wilderness mindset. The Promised Land requires an entirely different way of thinking. It requires the participation of the entire body to posses and to occupy the land. Those who are beginning their journey in God need to *feel, see,* and live on miracles, but that should only last for a season. Those who are matured and ready to live as sons and daughters of the kingdom know what they are supposed to do in spite of how they feel or what they don't see.

When we complete all of the above-mentioned 'transitions' and reach our final destination (which is the kingdom of God), and the true manifestation of the *ekklesia* is in every nation, then we will have an idea of how the church is actually supposed to look and function. It will take a few years to complete this process, so welcome to the journey!

Chapter 2
Understanding God's Order

Chapter 2

Understanding God's Order

The root cause of every problem we see today is a lack of understanding God's order. The Bible says He made all things beautiful and perfect. We messed things up. When we realign ourselves to God's order, life will become much easier.

The reason you are going through all kinds of trials and struggles that you never experienced before is because God is trying to redesign, redefine, and restructure your life according to His priority or order. We have been fighting Him because we have become used to our own ways and don't want to lose control of what is familiar to us.

Every time God spoke concerning man's purpose and identity, He put kingdom or dominion first. That's His order. When He created Adam, the first mandate (or assignment) He gave to him was to have dominion over the earth. To have dominion means to rule, manage, subdue, excel, maximize, bring to order, govern, and be fruitful. Anything else we do without following that first mandate is like pouring water into a pot that has a hole in the bottom. We keep pouring and put a lot of effort into it, but when we look inside, the pot is still empty.

That is the current situation of the church and our lives. God's order and design was intended to be extremely simple. When we put effort into what He wants us to be doing, we won't walk away feeling empty and disappointed; we will be filled with purpose.

When God brought the people of Israel to the Promised Land He made it very clear to them what He was expecting of them. He told them He wanted them to be a kingdom of priests and a holy nation (Exodus 19:6). Not to form singing groups in every village.

Jesus said the same thing to the church. When He said that He would build His church and the gates of hades would not prevail against it, He then gave the church dominion and told them that He would give us the keys of His kingdom, and that whatever we permitted on earth, heaven would also permit it, and whatever we did not permit on earth, heaven would also not permit (Matthew 16:19). That's very simple to understand, right?

As I stated before, Peter called us a chosen generation and a royal priesthood. Whenever God speaks of our purpose or identity, the ideas of royalty, kingdom, or dominion are always mentioned first. Even in Revelation when He talks about us, it says we have been made "kings and priests" (Revelation 1:6; 5:10). Without understanding dominion and kingdom, what we do as a church will not "stick" and we are stuck in a fruitless, endless cycle. The moment we leave the scene, things go back to the way they were before. Then we come back next Sunday morning to fill the pot again, forgetting that it has a hole in the bottom.

Jesus came preaching *the kingdom* first, not about an outpouring of the Holy Spirit. He preached and taught the kingdom for three-and-a-half years, then He said He would leave and the promise of the Father would come. If there is no kingdom, there will be no outpouring of the Holy Spirit.

When the people of Israel reached the Promised Land they established a kingdom, or nation, first. Then they built the temple, and the glory of the

Lord filled that temple. We try to work in the opposite order. We want the outpouring of the Holy Spirit, but we do not want the kingdom. The *Holy Spirit comes to help us administer His kingdom.* If there is no kingdom He will not come, it doesn't matter how loud we yell or holler.

The religious spirit always talks about what happened in the past and what is going to happen in the future, but says nothing about the present. There is only a constant repetition of what we did in the past. It is like sitting in a doctor's office waiting for our appointment. We are not at home anymore, but neither have we seen the doctor yet.

As a church we have been in that "waiting" period for about a hundred years. We could have restored hundreds of nations back to God in that time, if we only had the right understanding. This misconception came to the people of God primarily because of the influence from the religious spirit.

The church was hijacked by the religious spirit a long time ago. We didn't know that because we are blinded by it. It is the same way the religious leaders in Jesus' time were blinded by the religious spirit and didn't realize what they were missing. We look back at them and feel bad for them. They were the top spiritual leaders of their time; the world was perishing around them and they did not seem to care.

They thought that they were the most perfect and spiritual people on earth waiting for the Messiah, while He was walking right there in the midst of them. That is what the religious spirit will do to us too. God is doing something right in front of us, and we will miss it. I pray that we are not in this situation now.

People in every generation before us looked forward to living in our day. Without realizing it, we are living in the "future" to which every generation looked. Unfortunately, we still keep looking for some unknown future. They had great expectations for us and the days we are living in now, but it seems to me we are failing the great cloud of witnesses.

If you read almost all of the books about the kingdom that are out there now, they all promise good things for the future. This is because they are being influenced by the religious spirit. Jesus not only promises us a future kingdom, but a kingdom that is right here and now as well.

Later on in the book, I will be separating each verse from the four Gospels that pertain to the kingdom. I will put them all on the right timeline, showing when and where each of those verses are supposed to be fulfilled, and about whom each parable is referring (us, the present kingdom, the nation of Israel or the religious leaders of Jesus' time). I did this so you can have a clear understanding about the kingdom you are supposed to be living in right now. Once you have this understanding, you will not be swayed by every wind of doctrine that comes around, and you won't fall prey to the next Christian fad. (Ephesians 4:14).

We cannot separate our Christian life from the teaching of the kingdom. If we do, the result is a powerless and ineffective Christian life. We cannot separate church from the kingdom of God either. If we do, we get a religious organization or a social club where people have membership and pay a monthly fee.

There are others that teach that the church is the kingdom of God. I do not agree with that teaching because it is not scriptural. Please read *The Power and Authority of the Church* to gain a better understanding about this.

Without the message and power of the kingdom, the church has nothing to offer people or nations for the real life problems they are facing. When the church lost the correct outlook on kingdom awareness, it began to offer people heaven, canned food, and used clothes. Nobody in the Bible offered heaven to anyone through their preaching—not even Jesus.

Unfortunately, the enemy has fought fiercely to separate and estrange believers and the church from the kingdom of God. It was like the separation of church and state in our country, which should never have happened. In America, this occurred mainly because of confusion, heretical teachings about the kingdom, a lack of understanding, and a blinded church. Before Jesus' return He will restore the teaching and revelation of His kingdom to His church. You and I are in that process right now, and everywhere I go I hear people talking about the kingdom. That is very exciting news to me.

As with anything good, the enemy will take something that is true and twist it to make it look like a lie. He knows that once people start to believe a lie, it will be hard for them to change their mind or accept the truth. This is because most people will affirm that what they believe is the truth, even though it is a lie. When that happens, it will take a Damascus road experience to change their mindset. Many people look at the teaching of the kingdom as though it were bad. They try to stay away from it, maybe because of past abuse or someone's misinterpretation.

One wonderful pastor told me that we cannot take the kingdom message seriously in this day and age. We were talking about "bringing the enemies of Jesus to His footstool," and he said we can't take that seriously because of its few references! (There are actually *seven total*: six in the New Testament and one in the Old Testament). He had good intentions and I knew where he was coming from. He had a mindset that has been drenched in *"churchianity"* that has been ineffective for years.

I wanted to ask him, "Pastor, we have been preaching about being born again for hundreds of years, how many references of that do you see in the New Testament?" The answer to that is only twice (When Jesus talked to Nicodemus, the actual phrase appears twice, two times in John 3 and once in 1 Peter 1:23).

We have been specializing in revival and how to manufacture a revival culture in our churches for a long time too, but how many references do you see about revival in the New Testament? *Not even one.* We teach and preach about words like Trinity, and rapture, words, which are not even mentioned in the Bible once. The concepts are there but not the words. However, the moment we talk about the kingdom (the most preached subject by Jesus), the religious spirit has a problem with it. I wonder about that.

There are more than a hundred references to the kingdom—and many more verses that are referring to it directly—in the New Testament. So some are telling me not to preach and teach about the kingdom because there are not enough references to support its truth? Jesus told us to seek "first" the kingdom with our life, so why aren't we focusing on it? If that was the most important subject to Jesus and the early apostles, it should be the most important subject to the church today as well.

When we separate the kingdom of God from the teaching and life of the church, it is like having a nation without any proper government. Imagine a nation without a government, or a government that is corrupted. What would life look like in that nation? It would look like the body of Christ today.

In the body of Christ today, everyone is doing whatever they like, and teaching whatever they want to teach about. People start a church or ministry wherever and however they feel like they should. Chaos, confusion, disorder, and division are the result. In many parts of the world, all you need to start a church is four sticks and two tin sheets, one for the roof and the other one for the sign outside.

I have been to countries without a proper government. Government officials were corrupt, and in it for their own belly. They stole and robbed from their own nation and people; and as a result, these nations struggled in poverty, instability, and sometimes even civil wars. People were broke, tired, and oppressed. Anarchism ruled in the towns and cities. Everyone wanted to escape to a better country.

In many places, this is the picture of the body of Christ. They are tired of church and life here on earth, and waiting to escape to a better country, heaven. This is evidence of a state of anarchism in the body of Christ. Everyone is doing whatever seems right in their own eyes. The church lacks proper leadership and guidance.

Jesus envisioned His body to be *one* flock under *one* Shepherd. Now we have millions of little shepherds and dysfunctional bodies instead (John 10:16; 17:22-23).

Jesus did not teach the disciples how to cast out a demon, prophesy, pray for the sick, prepare a great sermon, or having a better life now. Instead, He taught them about His kingdom. In His kingdom there is healing, deliverance, power, and everything else we need. A king's power is in his kingdom. A nation's power is not in its leader, although he might control it. A nation's or kingdom's true power depends on its resources, government, size, and the productivity of its people.

We need to keep in mind that the church is the governing body of the kingdom of God. People, look at the church, scratch their heads, and say, "What's wrong with these people? They preach about unity and love, but do not practice. They cannot even get along with each other. Why should we join them?" The Lutheran, Methodist, Catholic, Seventh Day Adventist, and even Mormon groups function and work as one body within their denominations. The only ones who don't are the Pentecostals and the Charismatics though we claim to be the most holy and spiritual. That in itself should tell us there is something wrong with the system we are following.

Look at Pentecostal and Charismatics: No two believers get along well. We claim to be the most spiritual and anointed people on earth, and we are the most divided. There is something wrong with that picture. Just as every nation has a government, and every government has a body of people who governs its affairs, we need a proper government and administration.

I am convinced that two things must happen before Jesus can return to take His church. Otherwise the church will make Him look like a liar or a failure. Why? There are many verses in the gospel of John in which Jesus talked about the unity of the body of Christ.

> And other sheep I have which are not of this fold; them also I must bring, and they will hear My voice; and there will be one flock and one shepherd (John 10:16).

That is the heart of Jesus: *to see His body united as one flock under one Shepherd.* In John 17, Jesus prayed a powerful high priestly prayer:

> Now I am no longer in the world, but these are in the world, and I come to You. Holy Father, keep through Your name those whom You have given Me, that they may be one as We are (John 17:11).

> I do not pray for these alone, but also for those who will believe in Me through their word; that they all may be one, as You, Father, are in Me, and I in You; that they also may be one in Us, that the world may believe that You sent Me. And the glory which You gave Me I have given them, that they may be one just as We are one: I in them, and You in Me; that they may be made perfect in one, and that the world may know that You have sent Me, and have loved them as You have loved Me (John 17:20-23).

If these prayers don't mean anything, why would Jesus pray them? If the unity of His body was not meant to happen on earth, why would He pray for it? Some people say we will be all united in heaven, no matter which group we belong in here, but Jesus was not referring to unity in heaven. No. Those prayers must be answered on earth.

These verses will be fulfilled before His second coming. Then the gospel of the kingdom must be preached in all the world as a witness to all the nations, and then the end will come (Matthew 24:14). Until those two things happen, I do not believe Jesus is going to come back for His church.

All denominational walls must be leveled before Jesus will return. That will be a witness to the world of the power of God. Our unity will glorify God as nothing else could. In it, the world will see the love of the Father.

I have a word for the pastors and leaders of churches across the world. I have a couple of questions to ask you. Are we all working to establish God's kingdom on earth, though that may look differently in our personal understanding and perception? Are we all passionate about Jesus Christ? Saving souls? If we all trying to accomplish the same goal, then the goal of all the ministries we do is to extend and establish the kingdom of God, right? So why can't we all set aside our personal ambitions and work together in unity to accomplish that goal?

Can we all work together as one body and one flock instead of continuing divided, scattered, and ineffective? The world is making fun of us, whether we realize it or not. We are like the story of the "Emperor's New Clothes." He believed the lies of a tailor who told him he was fully clothed. Instead he was completely naked, and everyone could see his nakedness except him. So he kept riding on in his chariot, completely blind to the fact he had nothing on, while the public looked at him and laughed under their breath.

Don't you think that when we all work and put our resources together we will be able to accomplish things much faster and easier than we are now, as we try to do everything separately? You can still feel significant and your needs will be met; your personal vision and dreams will be fulfilled; and your family will be blessed. If you are concerned that giving up your control over your congregation will sabotage your salary or dream and you will be left with nothing, relax. That will never be the case.

There is a way we can work in unity as one body, and each of us will still feel significant and accomplish our dreams. Just like each member or part of our body is significant and has a unique role. To be honest, none of my body parts ever came to me complaining because they feel left alone or insignificant. I do not believe this will ever happen! Each part is uniquely designed and placed by the Creator. This will happen only when we have a revelation of the kingdom of God. We must have God's dream and His vision.

First of all, we need to come to a place where we decide that we are going to build God's kingdom and not our own personal kingdoms. In western culture, individualism and personal success is the mantra of every human being; I know it's hard to change our mindset. Some people even name ministries after themselves.

Everyone is focusing on their own personal success while the nation and the church is dying, and the body of Christ remains ineffective. The world is dying and going to hell. Does anyone care? God wants His church to be the next superpower, and when we put all of our resources together, we will be the largest economic force on earth.

We need to come to the conclusion that we are serving the same God, saved by the same blood, and sealed by the same Holy Spirit for the day of redemption. Can we humble ourselves as Jesus did when He gave up His glory and throne in heaven to come and save us? Can we give up our differences, and embrace each other as God in Christ Jesus has accepted and loved us, for a greater cause?

What if we lay down our personal agendas, pride, and ambition, and pick up the agenda of Jesus to make His dream our priority and His prayer come true? To see us all united as one body, one flock, and under one Shepherd.

We need to work together to fulfill the dream Jesus has. Actually, the purpose and function of the fivefold ministry gift is to unify the body. If you believe you are called into the fivefold ministry gifts mentioned in Ephesians 4:11-15, and you do not have a heart to unify the body of Christ, then there is something wrong with your understanding of your calling. You might be called to establish a business or an enterprise instead, and not lead the body of Christ.

To be honest, many of the present church leaders would make better business or corporate leaders than spiritual leaders. They have brought the principles and methods from the business world into the church. As a result, we have these enterprises which we call churches, which stand like islands in the midst of the ocean. We are not called to be on separate islands. We are one nation, a body of believers that should be fully engaged in every aspect of life in our society and nation. If we do that, do you think the devil will dare to accomplish his evil through our governments and other media he uses?

There are seven responsibilities attached to the fivefold minister mentioned in this passage.

> And He Himself gave some to be apostles, some prophets, some evangelists, and some pastors and teachers, for the *equipping of the saints for the work of ministry*, for the *edifying of the body of Christ*, till *we all come to the unity of the faith* and of the *knowledge of the Son of God*, to a *perfect man*, to the measure of the stature of the *fullness of Christ*; that we should no longer be children, tossed to and fro and carried about with every wind of doctrine, by the trickery of men, in the cunning craftiness of deceitful plotting, but, speaking the truth in love, may grow up in all things into Him who is the head—Christ (Ephesians 4:11-15).

Equipping the Saints for the Work of the Ministry: Ministry is not just prophesying, praying for the sick, and casting out demons. Joseph was a minister of God, but he was also the *prime* minister of a nation. Daniel was in ministry, but he was the head of the ministry of internal affairs in Babylon. A fivefold ministry gift has the responsibility to release every person into his or her calling — whatever it may be.

Edifying the Body of Christ: To edify means to encourage, exhort, and build up. A fivefold ministry gift must be doing these three things. They flow out of the gift itself.

Bringing ALL of Us to the Unity of Faith: Notice the word *all*? That means everyone! The entire body of Christ. This is a key responsibility of a fivefold ministry gift. They are supposed to serve the body by recognizing callings and gifts, and then placing people where they belong in the body so it functions well. This allows us to grow, manifesting the fullness of Christ: His glory, kingship, creativity: all of Him.

Not everybody who claims the title of a pastor or prophet or apostle is truly called to be one. Many call themselves to the ministry because of insecurity or the need to make a living. Everyone wants to feel significant. In many parts of the world there is no better way to feel worthwhile than being in ministry and have everyone else serve you. There are more people claiming to be apostles, prophets, and pastors today than at any other time in history.

In spite of this, there is no unity of faith or unity among the believers anywhere. That is proof that many of these people are not called into the fivefold ministry. They are wolves in sheep's' clothing devouring the sheep and exploiting them for their personal gain. They are serving their own belly and using the gullibility and ignorance of the believers to exploit them to build a personal empire. If you look at the end of these lives their empires came crumbling down before they even died. .

Bring Us the Knowledge of the Son of God: We need to be taught how to live as a son and daughter of God on earth today. Sin marred our perception and twisted how we see ourselves. As children of God, we should be so connected to Him that we function like Him. His will should be flowing out of our lives. People looking at us should see His image and likeness. Walking as children of light brings restoration all around us.

The Body Might Be a Perfect Man: Once fivefold ministry gifts manifest, their anointing will bring out the purpose of human beings and each individual. What and who is a perfect man? There were only two perfect men so far. One was Adam before the fall, and the second one is the last Adam, Jesus Christ. We need to be following their examples in how we live. Perfection is not referring to our dress code or our bodies, but the maturity of our spirits.

Reach and Manifest the Fullness of Christ: The teaching and training of the fivefold ministry gift is geared toward manifesting the fullness of Christ through the body of Christ. Who is Christ? He is the Creator, King, Judge, Healer, and so much more. Many only focus on the humility and poverty of Christ. Humility is His nature, and He became poor so that He could remove the curse of poverty from us. In the same way, He became sin so we can become the righteousness of God. Instead of maintaining a focus on those things, a fivefold ministry gift will present Christ as He is: a powerful King full of purpose, compassion, and strength. Doing this changes the perception of the body itself.

Doctrinal Stability: Today the body of Christ is swayed by every wind of doctrine because of the lack of true fivefold ministry gifts. Every three months a new revelation manifests and people run after it. Then someone else will come up with a new idea and believers will turn there. These folks are looking for answers. That's why they are running after all these new ideas, but they will only find true answers in the kingdom of God.

The fivefold ministers may have great charisma, excellent leadership skills, and can accomplish great things, but those qualities won't necessarily make you a leader in the body of Christ. If you want to be a leader in the body of Christ, the number one quality you are required to have is a revelation of His kingdom and a global picture of the church. Then you can work together with every other member in the body to accomplish the same goal God has for *all* of us.

The first revelation Jesus gave to the apostles was about His kingdom, not about grace, the cross, or revival. A fivefold minister without the revelation of the kingdom of God is not a true minister.

What is the dream Jesus has for His bride? His dream is that we will all become one as He, the Father, and the Holy Spirit are one (John 17:22-23).

He said that when we are united as one body, the world will know that the Father has sent Him. Until this happens, it doesn't matter how many mega churches we have and how many big crusades and music concerts we put together; they are all waste of money and time. We should use that money to feed the hungry or send some destitute children to school instead.

Jesus wants to see God's will accomplished on earth as it is in heaven. That's our common goal. That is God's main mission and agenda for this planet. There are ways and means for that goal to be accomplished.

There are a few goals the New Testament outlines for us to accomplish:

- To establish God's will on earth *as it is in heaven* (Matthew 6:10).

- That none should perish (Matthew 18:14).

- That this world and everything in it should be saved and redeemed (John 3:17; Romans 8:19-22).

- To disciple all nations (Matthew 28:19).

- To go into all the world (Mark 16:15).

- To preach the gospel of the kingdom in all the world in every nation (Matthew 24:14).

- To make His praise glorious (Psalm 66:2).

- To make the kingdoms of this world the kingdoms of our Lord Jesus Christ (Revelation 11:15).

- To fill the earth with His glory (Numbers 14:21; Psalm 72:19).

Everything we do as a church or a ministry should fit into one of these goals mentioned above. If you are not working to accomplish any of them, then you are not in true ministry. You are either in it for something else other than for God and His kingdom or you are mixed up about what your mission actually is. Take the time to assess your heart and your work before God, and begin again doing what you are actually called to do.

Too many ministries are functioning today that have nothing to do with God or His kingdom. They are part of a religious system, and their goal is just to grow. They want everyone to know their name and be a part of their organization. They are using God to accomplish fleshly dreams and plans, and are not part of the true church. Be sure you are not one of them.

Chapter 3
Dimension 1: God's Eternal Kingdom

Chapter 3

Dimension 1: God's Eternal Kingdom

Let's explore the wisdom and knowledge God has given me on the seven different dimensions and operations of the kingdom of God in different ages. Put your seat belt on and get ready to grasp everything God has for you. Let's start with the following verses.

> "Your kingdom is an everlasting kingdom, and Your dominion endures throughout all generations" (Psalm 145:13).

> "But the Lord is the true God; He is the living God and the everlasting King" (Jeremiah 10:10a).

> "For His dominion is an everlasting dominion, and His kingdom is from generation to generation" (Daniel 4:34b).

> "His kingdom is an everlasting kingdom, and all dominions shall serve and obey Him" (Daniel 7:27b).

Our God is a King and He has a kingdom. The above verses repeat the fact that the kingdom of our Lord God is an everlasting kingdom. These verses alone are sufficient to refute the kingdom-now-or-later philosophy that has been prevalent among some.

There was never a point in time in all of eternity when God's kingdom stopped operating or He took a break from exercising His dominion over His creation. This will never happen in the future either; so let us be clear on that and establish it once and for all. The kingdom and reign or dominion of our Lord is everlasting.

God is a King forever (Psalm 10:16). There is no time limit on His kingdom. God lives outside of time. We create unnecessary problems when we think of His kingdom as something that is yet to come or somewhere in the far future.

Though the intent of the Lord and His kingdom remains the same throughout all generations, the manifestation of it varies from generation to generation.

Every king must have a kingdom. Without a kingdom, no king can survive, and his kingship will not be valid. As with any other king and their kingdoms, our God wants His kingdom to grow and expand to other territories. It is the nature of every king to desire the expansion of His kingdom.

Let's step back in time and take a look with the eyes of our imagination into how things might have happened in eternity.

Years ago in eternity past there existed a glorious kingdom. The Great King who ruled this kingdom called His close senior associates for a very important meeting in His magnificent palace. His associates came to the meeting, knowing the King had something serious to share. Otherwise, He would not call them together for such a meeting.

They knew that whatever He was going to share would take place just as He said. The subject of the meeting was the expansion and prosperity of His kingdom. He said, "Everything I have is unlimited and never stops growing. I have purposed to expand My majestic kingdom to a new part of the universe and to create new planets." He shared what was in His heart, and everyone unanimously agreed to carry out the plan. They knew whatever the King planned would excel, and nothing would withstand His counsel.

This King and His kingdom worked a little differently than those we know on the earth. He has no opponent and His kingdom has no beginning or end. He is King Eternal. He has no lack of anything and does not depend on anyone to do anything. He does what He wills and His counsel stands forever. No one can ever thwart His purpose.

What made this particular meeting unique was that the King's only Son was called in to a special seat next to the Father. It was very clear that His Son was going to be a Key Player in this new venture. The Son paid keen attention to every detail His Father expressed regarding this new venture. He delighted in this new responsibility with which His Father was planning to entrust Him. The King said to His Son, "My beloved Son, I want You to design the planets and bring them into existence as I have spoken." The Son said to His Father, "Yes, Father, I am here to do Your pleasure."

> For by Him (the Son) all things were created that are in heaven and that are on earth, visible and invisible, whether thrones or dominions or principalities or powers. All things were created through Him and for Him (Colossians 1:16).

In John 1 we read, "All things were made through Him (the Son), and without Him nothing was made that was made" (John 1:3).

The King spoke specifically about a planet that would be called *Terras*. He said this planet would be unlike all the other planets He had created before. This one would be one of the most beautiful He had created so far. The King declared, "One of the specialties of this planet is that everything in it will praise and sing to Me. They will declare my works forever and ever.

It will be filled with my knowledge and glory. This planet will resemble My kingdom here in heaven in every way. My intent will be done on this planet as they are done here in My kingdom."

"I am going to give the management of this planet to no one other than my close associate, Lucifer. He is the worshiping prince and has a spirit of excellence, full of wisdom, so he will be in charge of my wealth, business, and all the development related to this planet. He and his echelons of angels, spirits, and other living creatures that assist him will inhabit this planet and ascribe glory and honor to me.

"Since Lucifer is in charge of the wealth and wisdom regarding the universe, I have given him permission to come in to my presence whenever I call the meetings of all the sons of God. I will also create other spirit beings and creatures to serve him in this kingdom."

This King is like no other kings, and He has a very special way of doing things. When He declares something, it comes into existence from that moment on. Nothing can stand in the way or annul what He said. The universe trembles at His voice and an innumerable number of angels stand ready to execute His orders.

The King declared His words, and His Son brought this special planet into existence. It was made by Him, and for Him, and through Him, though Lucifer was given the complete responsibility to manage it. The King paid very special attention to this planet, and everything in it was made by wisdom, understanding, and knowledge (Proverbs 3:19). He laid its foundation on water and then its atmosphere with water to protect it. It was one of the most beautiful places in the universe, and light shone from one end of the planet to the other end.

There was no need of any celestial lights. Light emanated from precious stones and lit up the skies. The atmosphere around this planet was specially protected by clouds and water. It did not need a sun or moon to give light.

Additionally, the brightness and glory of Lucifer illuminated it from one end to the other too, for his name meant "the light bearer." Because Lucifer was a different species than humans, the first earth's atmosphere in which he lived was very different than what we know today.

The earth we read about in Genesis 1:1-2 was not controlled by the solar system we have today. The earth at that time was full of darkness and void. God didn't create the sun, moon, and stars until the fourth day of creation.

Then the special day came when the King laid the foundation of this great planet. It was a great day of celebration. The sons of God were shouting for joy.

Job says,

> To what were its foundations fastened? Or who laid its cornerstone, when the morning stars sang together, and all the sons of God shouted for joy? (Job 38:6-7).

The King made a special throne for Lucifer. His throne was located in the span between this planet and heaven. Lucifer brought all the angels and other spirit beings that worked under him and made arrangements to praise and worship the King. It was a time of great joy and jubilation like no other time on earth and in heaven. The King rejoiced at His handiwork and saw His kingdom expanded to another level, making sure everything in this planet was an exact representation of His kingdom in heaven.

※※※

One of the qualities of a good king is that whenever he does something in a foreign country, he will replicate everything as it is in his kingdom. He will make sure that everything exactly represents the system and rule where His kingdom exists. His intention of expanding His kingdom is that those who see the work should know Him better, thereby increasing His popularity.

This is the story of the first earth we see in Genesis 1:1 where it says, "In the beginning God created the heavens and the earth." But in the very next verse it says, "The earth was without form, and void; and darkness was on the face of the deep. And the Spirit of God was hovering over the face of the waters." God wouldn't have created a dark and void world. So in the span of one verse the earth became dark, void, and flooded with water. How and why?

We do not know how long that world existed before the rebellion and revolt of Lucifer took place. He rebelled against God and tried to take over His kingdom. He was cut down to the ground and the world then was destroyed by a flood. That is the earth we see in Genesis 1:2.

Because of the fall and the following judgment, Lucifer became Satan, which means adversary, and the fallen spirit beings (not angels) that were on earth became demons and unclean spirits. They continued to roam on the earth, looking for a being to enter or for a place to rest, but they have never had the right or the authority to do so.

To know more about the fall of Lucifer and how the earth became like the one we see in Genesis 1:2, please read the book *Releasing Kings and Queens to their Original Intent: Kingdom Secrets to Restoring Nations Back to God, Volume III*. See the back of this book for ordering information.

The Restored Earth

The Deluvian Age

The Great King called for another meeting in heaven of His close associates and His one and only Son. His Son came with much anticipation of what His Father had to say concerning this planet Earth. He had been watching all that was happening there, and felt sorry for what had happened to Lucifer and the other spirit beings. The King was not willing to back down from His original plan concerning the earth. He said, "My kingdom would be established on the earth forever."

"So have I decided and so shall it be done."

"As long as I live, the earth shall be filled with My glory. My counsel shall stand."

"I will restore its beauty and glory and I will create another spirit being better than Lucifer and his fallen creatures. This being will be created in My own image and likeness; and with My own Spirit, I will give them life. Because they have come from Me and My Spirit gives them life, they will be My sons. They will not only serve me as Lucifer did, but their main job will be to make sure My kingdom is established on the earth as it was in the beginning. They will execute my will on the earth as it is in heaven, and I will give them power and authority over all that is there."

The King's words pleased everyone, and His Son felt a little uneasy about the whole picture of having other members in His family. The Son also knew in His innermost being that this family was going to cause Him great pain and He would have to be involved with this whole thing very closely. He said to the Father, "Father, why go through all this trouble? What if they also rebel?"

The Father replied, "I know, My Son; I have provided a ransom and planned everything well. I have prepared a Lamb before the foundation of the world."

The Son said, "Father, I am here to do Your will, whatever it may be. Whenever You need any help in doing anything on the earth, You can call Me and I will go to any extent to help You with these new beings—even if I have to go to the earth and live among them and lay down My own life for them."

The Re-creation of the Earth

In Genesis 1:2, the Hebrew words say that the earth became void and empty. Nothing God creates is empty, void, shapeless, or chaotic. The surface of the earth was flooded and covered with water.

If you go to some places on the earth you can actually see that the surface formation of the earth is just like those we see under the ocean. In Colorado Springs, Colorado, in the United States, there is a place called the Garden of the Gods. It is an amazing place full of red sandstone. The rocks look like they had been under water for thousands of years.

We do not know how long the earth remained flooded. I believe it was for millions of years. The pre-Adamic world was buried under the water, and there are fossils and remains that scientists have discovered that are thought to be millions of years old. Oil and precious metals that we mine from the ground date back to the debris of the world that existed before Adam. As the Word says, He makes all things work together for our good. Out of the destruction, He brought something beautiful.

The Great King looked at the earth and said, "Let there be light." As we know, whatever He declared manifested immediately. Why did He have to create light first? Because He did not create the sun, moon, and stars until the fourth day. As we know, the earth was filled with darkness. The Hebrew word for darkness is *choshek*[1] (kho-shek'), meaning the dark; hence (literally) darkness; and figuratively, misery, destruction, death, ignorance, sorrow, and wickedness.

The word *darkness* also means ignorance. God created light, and the Hebrew word for *light* is *owr*[2] which has more than one meaning as well. It can be:

---

[1] James Strong, "2822. Choshek," Biblehub.com, accessed November 26, 2018, https://biblehub.com/hebrew/2822.htm.

[2] James Strong, "Genesis 1:1 (KJV)," Blue Letter Bible, accessed November 26, 2018, https://www.blueletterbible.org/lang/lexicon/lexicon.cfm?t=kjv&strongs=h216.

a) the light of day

b) the light of heavenly luminaries (the moon, the sun, the stars)

c) daybreak, dawn, the morning light

d) daylight

e) lightning

f) the light of a lamp

g) the light of life

h) the light of prosperity

i) the light of instruction

j) the light of one's face (figuratively)

k) or Yahweh as Israel's Light

In the New Testament we read that God commanded the light to appear out of darkness:

> For it is the God who commanded light to shine out of darkness, who has shone in our hearts to give the light of the knowledge of the glory of God in the face of Jesus Christ (2 Corinthians 4:6).

We also read phrases like, "we are the light of the world," "let your light shine," and "Your light has come." *Light* can also mean wisdom, glory, knowledge, or brightness. The first light God created was *out of* darkness, not from the sun, moon, or stars. Those bodies were not created until the fourth day. The new earth and new heaven will be lit by the rightness of Jesus, and not by terrestrial stars. God separated night and day, dark and light, wisdom and ignorance.

In six days God recreated the whole earth and made it a beautiful place. God looked at what He had made and said it was good. Whatever God makes or creates is always good.

Chapter 4

Dimension 2: The Kingdom of God in the Garden of Eden

Chapter 4

Dimension 2: The Kingdom of God in the Garden of Eden

After God reestablished and restored the earth and put everything in order, He decided to create man in His image and likeness to rule and to reign on earth on His behalf. The Lord God came down and planted a garden in the east and He put the man in it to take care of it. Man's responsibility was to rule the earth and the rest of creation. He had total authority over every creature and thing God has made on earth.

> Then God said, 'Let Us make man in Our image, according to Our likeness; let them have dominion over the fish of the sea, over the birds of the air, and over the cattle, over all the earth and over every creeping thing that creeps on the earth.' So God created man in His own image; in the image of God He created him; male and female He created them. Then God blessed them, and God said to them, 'Be fruitful and multiply; fill the earth and subdue it; have dominion over the fish of the sea, over the birds of the air, and over every living thing that moves on the earth' (Genesis 1:26-28).

This was the Creator's intention for human beings. It is very important to notice that God never mentioned anything about heaven or going to heaven to Adam, nor about worship or singing. Adam's life and purpose was totally connected to the earthly realm. He was supposed to rule the earth on God's behalf.

The garden of Eden was the most luxurious place on earth. It was the visible manifestation of the invisible kingdom of God. Man had been appointed to manage the earth and establish His kingdom. God's will was done in Eden as it was in heaven. Life in the garden was the same as life in heaven. That is God's original intent for all of us. That is what Jesus taught us to pray in the Lord's Prayer. God did not create man to live or reign in heaven. He was created to live and reign on earth (Psalm 115:16). He never changed His mind concerning man's purpose.

There is no sickness in heaven, and there was no sickness in the garden. There is no poverty in heaven, and there was none in the garden. There is no curse or sorrow in heaven and there was no curse or sorrow in the garden. There is no death in heaven; and as long as Adam and Eve lived in the garden, death had no power over them. That was (and still is) kingdom living.

Man's responsibility was to have dominion or rule the earth on behalf of God. He was the direct representation of God to the rest of creation. Whatever Adam would do on earth was as same as God would do directly. He was a king over the whole earth. Man had immense potential and capacity. When other creatures saw man, it was as though they were looking at God, because he was the son of God (Luke 3:38).

The Fall of Man

For some reason, the King did not remove Lucifer (satan) and his fallen spirit beings from the planet. They had access to it and waited for an opportunity to usurp it. They planned a coup to take it over once again.

Satan noticed the new changes that had taken place on the earth. He was not happy about the relationship God had with man and the position He gave him. He became jealous and came up with a plan to break that relationship. The only way he could do that was to get Adam and Eve to disobey God's commandment. Eve was deceived by the enemy and ate the fruit that she was not supposed to eat, and Adam ate it with her.

Satan was jealous of mankind for two primary reasons: God had made them in His own image and likeness, and second, this man had taken his place and his kingdom. He believed that if he did not destroy man in the beginning, he would lose total access to his old kingdom (earth). Satan also saw that God loved mankind. What better way to exact revenge than to destroy them?

I believe there was some kind of challenge set between Lucifer and God behind the scenes. Lucifer challenged God, saying, "This species you are creating would worship me if you created them with a free will and gave them an opportunity." The All-Knowing God accepted the challenge and created us with a free will, knowing full well what it would cost Him in the end.

Because of the challenge, two special trees were placed in the garden. The Tree of Life belonged to the Great King and the second one belonged to Satan; it was called the Tree of the Knowledge of Good and Evil. Mankind would experience the consequences of whichever tree they ate of first. They would also inherit the nature of the source of that tree. The first one led to life, and the second one to death.

Satan crafted a cunning plan to take over the earth. He knew if he was to maintain the right to be on the earth, he had to wrench it from this man somehow, as the King had given the man all the authority, power, and dominion over the earth (Psalm 8:6-8).

Satan and his demons could not enter into humans because the glory of God was protecting them. Even today, anything that wishes to defeat man has to make man willfully disobey God's Word first. The devil knew this very well, and that is why he did not come for a face-to-face confrontation with the man. If he had, man could have easily defeated the devil. Instead, he disguised himself as the serpent in order to tempt and deceive man to disobey God's Word. The devil did not defeat man until man first disobeyed God's Word. This is still true today. (To know more about this subject, please read my book, *Sin, Flesh, and the Devil*).

Through deception, Adam and Eve ate from the tree that represented the devil. As a result, two seeds, kingdoms, and ways of life were created on earth. One was God's way and the other was Satan's. One was God's kingdom and the other the kingdom of darkness. Two kinds of human races began to operate on earth: one was the righteous seed and other was wicked (Genesis 3:15).

Satan's plot worked this time and he stole the legal authority over the earth from mankind, influencing the sons and daughters of men to worship him instead of worshiping the Great King. He began to afflict the human race with all sorts of evil to drive them away from relationship with the Great King.

Once they disobeyed God they lost the glory of God they had previously reflected as well as their dominion. At that time, Satan and his demons legally received the authority to enter into humans. Since then, there have been two lineages of people on earth. The seed of the righteous and seed of the wicked one—sons of the light and sons of darkness. The Bible uses different terminologies to describe these two groups, and each one produced its corresponding seed: good or evil. The battle for dominion began between them, and is still going on today.

This battle will only end when Jesus defeats the last enemy, which is death (1 Corinthians 15:26) and throws Satan into the lake of fire in the final judgment (Revelation 20:10).

DIMENSION 2: THE KINGDOM OF GOD IN THE GARDEN OF EDEN

Through the help of the humans, Satan began to rebuild his kingdom on this earth. Anyone who yields to the devil becomes his instrument in fulfilling his desire, will, and intentions. In turn, they reveal his nature.

That is why when the devil tempted Jesus, he took Jesus to a high mountain and showed Him all the kingdoms and glory of the world, saying that all that had been delivered unto him and he could give them to whomever he willed.

Then the devil, taking Him up on a high mountain, showed Him all the kingdoms of the world in a moment of time. And the devil said to Him, 'All this authority I will give You, and their glory; for this has been delivered to me, and I give it to whomever I wish. Therefore, if You will worship before me, all will be Yours' (Luke 4:5-7).

After man sinned, God came down and walked through in the garden, but man and woman were hiding from God. They committed sin against God, which took away the confidence they previously possessed. They could no longer stand in the presence of God.

Fear, shame, and self and sin-consciousness came upon them as the result of their sin and they lost the glory of God. God could not keep them in the garden, which was His kingdom, and He made them leave it. Man not only lost the relationship with God, but he also lost all the provision God had given him. He lost the kingdom of God.

Sin affected man's relationships on five different levels.

1) His relationship with God was broken, and as a result it affected:

2) His relationship with himself

3) His relationship with others

4) His relationship with nature

5) His relationship with heaven and the spirit world

Now man was left on his own to provide for himself. He could no longer expect the lush provision around him to meet his needs. Instead, he had to work to meet his own needs. He was cast out of the kingdom of God, and all the things that came with the kingdom were lost too. His food, shelter, and all the material blessings were gone (Matthew 6:33).

As man lost the kingdom of God and was put outside the garden, sin entered the earth too; and with sin came the curse, sickness, poverty, and death. But God loved this man so much that He was willing to give up His only Son to redeem us.

Four Needs of Man since the Fall

Ever since man fell and was exiled from the garden, our spirit man has been longing for its homeland ever since (Hebrews 11:13-15). Every human being is searching for four major things. Though Adam was perfect before the fall and He had the most intimate relationship with God, it was not enough for man to live on this earth. God recognized those needs and met them for Adam. Let's see what those needs are.

1: A Place or Country

Just like each seed needs a particular soil, every human being needs a suitable place to live and fulfill his or her purpose. God knew that man needed a particular environment in order to fulfill his purpose, so He created the garden with exactly what man needed.

> The Lord God planted a garden eastward in Eden, and there
> He put the man whom He had formed (Genesis 2:8).

Because of sin, man lost this environment where his spirit really belongs. We are all on a search for this country, place, or a house so our spirit will feel at home. Whether you are a believer or unbeliever, your spirit is yearning for this lost country. Many people migrate from one country to another, from one city to another, thinking if they just reach that new place they will be better off. But once they get there, they find out it was only mirage. The grass truly wasn't greener on the other side; it just looked that way from a distance. Their spirit did not feel at home, so they continue to search.

Others will move from one city or town to another, thinking they will find that feeling of "home" there. Still others are looking for that perfect house or neighborhood. It doesn't matter where you live. Until you rediscover the kingdom of God, your spirit will never feel at home, even if you live in the Promised Land (Hebrews 11:13-16).

It's in the heart of man to look for luxury. The garden of Eden was luxurious, but it had something unique about it. The glory and the presence of the Lord is what made the whole difference! Luxury without God's presence will not satisfy your longing. You can live in the most opulent surroundings on earth and still be unhappy and unfulfilled.

2: Person

It doesn't matter how close you are to God, how anointed you are, and how much you realize God loves you, your heart will still long to have an intimate relationship with another human being. The more you realize how much God loves you, the more you want to share that love with someone else. Love is not love unless we share it with someone. That is the *side effect* of love.

Adam had a very close relationship with God; they fellowshipped every day. But God recognized that their relationship was not enough for Adam. Adam needed a human companion who would be a helpmate for him. It was God's idea. Unless you are given the gift of celibacy in His kingdom, you are designed by God to be in relationship. Even then you will need friends and coworkers.

> And the Lord God said, "It is not good that man should be alone; I will make him a helper comparable to him" (Genesis 2:18).

We are created for relationships. Our hearts are longing and searching for a meaningful relationship with at least with one other person with whom we feel accepted, appreciated, and loved. Relationships in which we are free to share our heart and give and receive love. If we do it right, God intended for this to happen in a marriage relationship, but unfortunately most people mess it up because they do not get married for the right reason.

Many people are damaged and wounded. When they get married, they expect the other person to fill the holes in their soul. When those expectations are not met, fights erupt for personal rights. Each one wants the other to meet their needs—and no one wants to give in. The result is that they end that relationship and move to the next one, which normally will also fail because of the same issues.

3: Purpose

The closer you are to God, the more you will begin to realize His purpose and plan for your life. You are not supposed to seclude yourself from everyone around you, live in a cave, and commune with God day and night. God sent you here to fulfill an assignment, just like He gave Adam an assignment to tend and keep the garden.

> Then the Lord God took the man and put him in the garden of Eden to tend and keep it (Genesis 2:15).

We all need a reason for our existence, and each of us was created for a specific reason. Until we discover that reason and fulfill it, we will never be happy. I was recording a TV program in a studio, and my host asked me, "What do you do for living? You look pretty happy." I responded, "There is nothing more enjoyable and satisfying than fulfilling your purpose." People who do not know their purpose or walk in their calling need to do other things to make them happy because the work they do is just drudgery. They are not enjoying it, but have to do it to survive. God wants us to live life to the fullest, not just stay in survival mode!

I have written an entire book on how to discover your purpose, calling, and gifts. Please refer to them to find out more about those subjects.

4: Power

Everyone is looking for power. People are willing to pay any amount of money to have power over their circumstances. However, so many people go to the wrong source to find power, and at the end of their lives, it destroys them. There is only one true Source of power in this universe—that is God (Psalm 62:11).

If you are a believer who is Spirit-filled, there is power in you; but God's power does not manifest the same way through everyone. That's one of the areas in which the church has messed things up and limited the Spirit of God. We all love and want the gifts of the Holy Spirit, but no one wants the Holy Spirit Himself. When His gifts are operating through someone, we all get excited and think that person is a superhero, instead of recognizing the workings of the Holy Spirit in all of us, and glorifying God as we should.

Think of it this way: We all have gifts and we give gifts to others. But those gifts are not who we are; they are just a small part of our life. The same thing is true with the Holy Spirit. The Holy Spirit is a person and He is much bigger than His gifts. He can anoint a person to govern a nation, like He did with Joseph, David, and others. He can anoint you to be the best musician in the world. He can anoint someone to become a great scientist or an inventor. We need to see the Big Picture and not put God in a box.

There is no limit to what the Holy Spirit can do through a person, but because we lack understanding in this area, the church has become narrow-minded and ineffective. Everyone is running after the gifts and they think if they don't have one of the nine gifts mentioned in 1 Corinthians 12, there is something wrong with them.

The church has been divided, mainly based on the misunderstanding of the operation of the Holy Spirit. The Pentecostals and the Charismatics will not accept the other groups because they do not speak in tongues like we do. We forget that the other groups are better with some things than we are; and that the Holy Spirit is using them to do that. One of my favorite verses in the Bible is:

> There are diversities of gifts, but the same Spirit. There are differences of ministries, but the same Lord. And there are diversities of activities, but it is the same God who works all in all (1 Corinthians 12:4-6).

The above verse says there are diversities of gifts, ministries, and activities. It seems to me the Father, Son, and the Holy Spirit give different types of gifts to people. I believe that if the Holy Spirit has gifts, then the Father and Son also have gifts. The Father's gifts are those people receive at birth, the natural gifts or the gifts of our body. The gifts of the Son are the fivefold ministry gifts and gifts of our soul mentioned in Romans 12.

Salvation

In eternity past, the Great King called another important meeting in heaven. He was not willing to give up that easily and give away His sons and daughters on earth. Now He was dealing with His own family. He wanted to redeem mankind and restore his relationship with Him. He knew the job would be tough, but it had to be done. He knew that He could not violate His own principles. He had said that whoever sins must die. Now, either He had to kill this new race or someone had to die in their place.

He Himself could not go to the earth because earth is a physical world and He is a Spirit. Only a person who had a physical body could live on the earth. He cannot die because He is an everlasting King. It had to be a human being like Adam who would be able to go to the earth and die on behalf of the humans. Before he died in their place, he had to teach and demonstrate the truth of the kingdom to the people on earth. He had to show them what it meant to live in His kingdom.

He said, "Whom shall I send and who shall go for Me?" (Isaiah 6:8). There was a moment of silence. Then His Son spoke up, "Father, remember what I said? If You ever need any help with this earth, I will do anything." He continued by saying, "I will go; send Me." The King looked at His Son and whispered, "I knew that, My Son. I knew that one day I would have to let You go for a special mission like this. I knew that for a moment I would have to hide My face from You and forsake You. For a moment I will have to forsake you, but with great mercy I will restore You. I will be with You all the way." The King was happy because He was getting His family back, yet He was overwhelmed to let His Son go through the pain and suffering He would have to endure in order for it to happen.

The King knew there needed to be a great price paid to restore the man to his original position. He told His Son, "You must die in their place, so I can fellowship with them again. I want to fellowship with them, but they can't see or understand Me because they are so blinded by the darkness in them. Son, I am sending You to earth to become a human and pay the price for their freedom."

The King went on to say, "I want My kingdom to be restored. As you go, My Son, tell the people to prepare to enter My kingdom once again. Show them what it is like to live in My kingdom. Teach them what they must know and do to see, enter, and inherit My kingdom. After You come back from accomplishing Your part, I will send the Comforter (Governor-General of the kingdom) to be with them and to be *in* them to enable them to live in My kingdom and truly do My will.

"This time, My kingdom is going to be invisible, and only those who believe in You, My Son, will be able to see, enter and inherit it. I will forgive those who believe in You and Your death on the cross and resurrection for their sin. I will qualify them to enter My kingdom."

"Wherever two or three are gathered in Your name, I will go and dwell in their midst. Those who believe in You, upon them I will pour out My Spirit to enable them to live victoriously. They will come together to administer My kingdom; and those groups will be called *ekklesia*." They will be a group of people who are called out to represent the kingdom and execute the will of the Great King on this earth."

"Through *ekklesia* I will accomplish my purpose on the earth. It will be the only visible form of My kingdom for a while. It will be the embassy and the governing body of My kingdom, and I will give them My power and authority over all the power of the enemy. Nothing shall by any means hurt them. Those who are trained by the *ekklesia* will go forth and preach the gospel of My kingdom and bring more people into the fold."

"*Ekklesia* will be the only force on earth that can thwart and destroy the power of the enemy and keep him where he belongs. They will go forward in My power and take new territories for Me until the whole earth is filled with My glory, as it was in the beginning. Then, at the end, I will destroy the enemy forever and cast him into the lake of fire."

"You, My Son, after You finish the works I have given You to do, will sit at My right hand until I make Your enemies Your footstool through the *ekklesia*." (This particular Old Testament Scripture is the most repeated in the New Testament; it is mentioned seven times.)

"Everything depends on how My *ekklesia* will train the people to live in My kingdom. The more they speak the language of My kingdom and understand its culture and how it functions, the more victorious and successful they will be. My kingdom will be a spiritual kingdom, and the natural people will not be able to see, enter, or understand it."

"This time, I am going to keep satan on the earth for a time, but I will rule and reign My kingdom in the midst of My enemies. No matter what he tries, he will not be able to thwart My purpose. I will build My kingdom and the gates of hell shall not prevail against it. Any person who believes in You, My Son, will have the Comforter to come and dwell in them to establish My kingdom. He will empower that believer to execute My plan as I originally designed. That way, My original intent for the earth will come to pass and My kingdom shall be established there forever."

There was a prophecy in the book of Genesis which said that the seed of the woman will crush the head of the serpent and he will bruise the heel of the seed of the woman (Genesis 3:15). Ever since that prophecy was declared by the King, the human race began to look forward to the arrival of that Seed. Many myths and superstitions began to surface, as people tried to figure out who that seed would be. The devil tried to impersonate that seed and deceive humanity that he was the real seed many times in history. Thus various religions, dictatorships, and myths were born.

The enemy also began to comb through the generations to identify that seed and destroy it before He would grow up and crush his head. He began to fight every woman and male child on earth. He inspired many kings to destroy male children from their kingdoms, like Pharaoh did in Egypt and Herod did after the birth of Jesus.

Ever since God released that prophecy in Genesis 3:15, He has been preparing the earth and the world for the fulfillment of it. Everything else His did from that time forward was geared toward fulfilling that one single prophecy. He began to choose individuals, made different covenants with man, and eventually established the nation of Israel to bring that Seed to earth. In the following pages we are going to see how God's plan was unfolded through the pages of history.

The Restoration of Man

After the fall of Adam, the kingdom of the Great King ceased to work directly on the earth, even though He was still the owner of it. The devil became the ruler of the earth and its systems. The King was not happy about it. He wanted His kingdom reestablished on the earth so it would operate as it did in heaven again. People began to multiply on the earth and the enemy was successful in influencing them to worship him instead of the King. The King also had His people on earth to accomplish His purpose until the time came for Him to reestablish His kingdom.

With the partnership of humans, Satan began to build his own kingdom too. He helped man make things that would satisfy man, so that man was sated. The devil's intent was for man to trust in those things and be happy so he would never have to on, or look for, God again. But God in His mercy did not leave us in that state forever. He had a plan to restore His kingdom. We could not enter His kingdom as sinners. We had to get rid of our sin before we could enter His kingdom.

God had to regain His dominion over the earth. He had to defeat Satan, who had set himself up as a king and was ruling. The devil was holding the whole human race in captivity. That is why the Bible says that Jesus came to set the captives free. God had prophesied about defeating and dethroning the enemy. He said, "And I will put enmity between you and the woman, and between your seed and her Seed; he shall bruise your head, and you shall bruise His heel" (Genesis 3:15).

The seed of the woman God was referring to was Jesus. Ever since the prophecy was revealed, Satan began to fight against women and her seed. Satan was nervous and did not want to lose his ground; neither could he recognize which woman and whose seed God would use that to fulfill that prophecy. It took almost four thousand years for that prophecy to be fulfilled.

> But when the fullness of the time had come, God sent forth His Son, born of a woman, born under the law (Galatians 4:4).

God sent His only Son to the earth to die for our sins, and whoever believes in Him becomes a child of God, qualified to enter the kingdom of God. That is why Jesus came with the message of the kingdom and said that if we seek His kingdom and righteousness first, all the things we needed in our lives would be added to us. God has been in the process of restoring His dominion and man's rightful position. It will be fully restored only when Jesus establishes His throne in New Jerusalem and rules the entire earth. Until then, His direct reign will be limited, but His sovereign reign is over all—for all the time.

Chapter 5
Dimension 3: Kingdom of God through the Lives of the Patriarchs

Chapter 5

Dimension 3: Kingdom of God through the Lives of the Patriarchs

Once Adam lost dominion over the earth, God began to use individuals to accomplish His kingdom purposes: Noah, Abraham, Isaac, Jacob, Moses, and David are some that God used. They were His representatives (or ambassadors) on earth.

Sometime they were the only righteous bloodline anywhere on the entire earth. They had to fight the fight of faith, and there was no church or fellowship group, social media, resources, or anything like that to help them. With all the support systems we have today, it's hard to imagine how we still struggle sometimes to keep going in our journey. When that happens, we need to remember the fathers of our faith who were lonely and stood alone for God and did not back down. They were steadfast in their kingdom purpose.

God used these individuals to accomplish His will and prove to the rest of the world and its kingdoms that He is the King and reigns over all. No one could defeat or destroy these people because God Almighty was their strength and protection. Those who touched them were touching God Himself. He released His wealth and wisdom to them to expand His kingdom on earth.

God revealed some aspect of His kingdom to and through every human being He ever used. He told Adam to have "dominion": that's a kingdom word. Let's look a little closer into how the King and His kingdom operated through some of these Old Testament saints.

Abraham

When God called Abraham from the land of Ur, He gave him promises and made a covenant with him. Genesis 12:1-3 says, "Now the Lord had said to Abram: 'Get out of your country, from your family and from your father's house, to a land that I will show you. I will make you a great nation; I will bless you and make your name great; and you shall be a blessing. I will bless those who bless you, and I will curse him who curses you; and in you all the families of the earth shall be blessed.'"

Abraham is the father of the nation of Israel and the father of our faith for all believers in Christ Jesus. It is important to notice that God called him to give him a land. Why land? Because every king needs a kingdom, and every kingdom needs land to establish it. God gave the garden of Eden to Adam (land). God rebuked kings and kingdoms for Abraham's and his children's sake and blessed him with abundance.

Operating God's kingdom always requires land. Even in the millennium, the capital New Jerusalem requires land to function so it will come down to the earth. Every covenant, call, and purpose of God is connected to a land. I have written about the importance of land in the book *Releasing Kings and Queens to Their Original Intent*.

There are seven promises God gave to Abraham in Genesis 12:2-3

1) I will make you a great nation.

2) I will bless you.

3) I will make your name great.

4) You shall be a blessing.

5) I will bless those who bless you.

6) I will curse him who curses you.

7) In you all the families of the earth shall be blessed.

All seven promises are geared toward expanding God's kingdom; they are terrestrial or earthly in nature. There was nothing super-spiritual, or about going to heaven or what will happen when he gets to heaven about it. God wanted to bless Abraham; and in turn, He wanted him to be a blessing to the entire earth. It was crystal clear what God expected of Abraham and what He wanted to do through him.

Why would God want to make Abraham a great nation? Because He wanted to accomplish His kingdom purposes on the earth through the nation that would be coming from Abraham's family. Through Abraham, God established the nation of Israel. They were the most blessed nation on earth and became a blessing to the entire earth in every facet of their existence.

Abraham was God's chosen vessel. The first thing He promised Abraham was a land and then to make a great nation through him. That was God's idea from the beginning. He established the first nation in Eden with just two people: Adam and Eve. That was the kingdom of God in visible form on earth.

God also promised Abraham a seed, through which the Seed of the woman that was prophesied in Genesis 3:15 would come. Though Abraham had many natural seeds, there was only one promised seed, which was Isaac, who was born through Sarah (Romans 9:7-9).

Through the descendants of Abraham, God established the nation of Israel. God blessed Abraham in every way. He made his name great by allowing him to become the father of three world religions: Judaism, Islam and Christianity. Every generation since knows who Abraham is. He became a blessing to humanity. All the families of the earth are blessed by Him. That was ultimately done through His Seed, Jesus Christ. God also promised him that kings would come out of his loins (Genesis 17:6). We, the church, are also called a nation. The apostle Peter called the church a holy nation. God wants to bless the entire world through us, just as He blessed the entire earth through Abraham.

How did God reveal His kingdom to Abraham? There are many ways, but I will mention a few of them here. Abraham's name means the father of many nations. His name itself proves that he is a king. God called him out to establish a nation and to bring forth a generation of kings and priests. The best example of Abraham's life representing the kingdom of God is through the parable Jesus shared about the mustard seed and the kingdom.

Abraham was a single man when God called him. God promised him that through him *all* the families of the earth will be blessed. Notice the word *all*, when God says *all* it means everything. The parable of the mustard seed explains that though it is one of the smallest seeds, it grows to be a tree, and the birds of the air come and nest in its branches.

Jesus was revealing one of the mysteries of how the kingdom grows. Just like that single seed blessed all the creatures around it, Abraham was a single man that blessed the whole world. This is an example of how the kingdom of God also starts small but grows to influence everything around it.

God also revealed His kingdom to Abraham when he had the encounter with Melchizedek, king of Salem. *Melchizedek* means the king of righteousness, and *salem* means peace (Hebrews 7:2). He is the king of righteousness of a place called peace. That is interesting because Paul wrote that "the kingdom of God is not eating and drinking, but righteousness and peace and joy in the Holy Spirit" (Romans 14:17). *Righteousness, peace and joy in the Holy Spirit is the culture of the kingdom.*

Through the encounter with Melchizedek, God revealed Himself to Abraham as a King, teaching him about His kingdom with its culture and economy in one revelation. They had communion and Abraham gave a tithe of everything to Melchizedek.

Right after he had this encounter with Melchizedek, the king of Sodom (representing this world's system) came to meet Abraham. He asked him to return all the people but keep all the goods he had taken in battle. Abraham had had a revelation of kingdom economy by now, so he said, "'I have raised my hand to the Lord, God Most High, the Possessor of heaven and earth, that I will take nothing, from a thread to a sandal strap, and that I will not take anything that is yours, lest you should say, "I have made Abraham rich"' (Genesis 14:22-23).

Melchizedek was a king-priest of the Most High God (Genesis 14:18), just like every believer in Christ is in this day and age. Only when we have the proper understanding of the kingdom of God are we able function as kings and priests on earth.

As I mentioned earlier, before God does anything major He reveals His kingdom. Though Abraham was called, God had not yet made a covenant with him. After he received the revelation of the kingdom, Abraham was ready to enter into covenant with God. In Genesis 15 we read about it. The same pattern can be seen in the New Testament. Before Jesus made the new covenant with us, He taught His disciples and the people of Israel about His kingdom.

Through Abraham came Isaac. Isaac had two sons, Esau and Jacob. God chose Jacob, and he had twelve sons. He changed his name to Israel. One of his sons, Joseph, was sold as a slave to Egypt. After many years, God brought a famine in the land of Israel. Meanwhile

Joseph was on his own in Egypt and endured many trials. Amazingly, he was eventually promoted to one of the highest positions, becoming one of the rulers of the country. When his family needed help, they travelled to Egypt to get food, and there was Joseph, placed by God Himself and waiting for them.

Joseph brought his father, along with his brothers and their families out of Palestine to Egypt. At first there were only seventy of them, but they began to multiply and became a threat to a later pharaoh after Joseph died. After four hundred and thirty years (Exodus 12:40), God brought His people out of Egypt to take them to the land that He had promised their father Abraham and establish them as the nation of Israel. God used Moses to deliver them out of Egypt, and after forty years journeying in the wilderness, they entered the Promised Land.

God used the nation of Israel to reveal Himself to all the nations of the world. God promised Abraham a land. How many times did God talk about this land? And why land?

Every king knows—and our God is a King—that without land it is impossible to have a kingdom. Land or territory is necessary to exercise spiritual and natural jurisdiction over a region. Since the fall of man, Satan had taken dominion over the earth and set up his own dark kingdom. Since that time, God had been trying to regain that dominion and give it back to His children.

The Abrahamic covenant is vitally important because everything else God ever did is based on that covenant and the promises He gave to Abraham. Everything else was an expansion or add-on to that covenant. Later we will learn about David and how he was a seed of Abraham, whom God anointed as the second king of Israel. I want you to keep one thing in mind for now: God promised Abraham a land and a seed. The same God made a covenant with David and promised him a throne (2 Samuel 7:16), a throne that would never cease; and it was not just any throne. It was the throne of the Lord upon which the future Messiah would sit and rule the entire earth and establish His kingdom.

It was to Jesus that the Father would give the whole kingdom, throne, and land, as well as the authority to rule the nations (Revelation 12:5).

We need to see the progression God made in establishing His kingdom on earth. To Abraham He promised a land, to David a throne, and to Jesus the whole kingdom and all the nations. That is why the New Testament begins with this verse:

> The book of the genealogy of Jesus Christ, the Son of David, the Son of Abraham (Matthew 1:1).

Before Jesus, there wasn't much teaching or preaching about the kingdom. Only people like David and Daniel had revelation of it and talked about it prophetically. It was Jesus who came and began to openly teach, preach, and show people what life in His kingdom was supposed to look like and what that meant. He is the first One who gave command to His disciples to take His kingdom message to the ends of the earth. He took the veil off the kingdom message and invited people from anywhere to enter and experience it.

Until Jesus, access to the kingdom was limited only to the nation of Israel. They were the only chosen people who could experience and benefit from it. They were supposed to share it with the other nations, but they kept it for themselves instead.

Whenever a king or a kingdom tries to occupy or colonize a new territory, the first thing they do is get a piece of land so they can set up an outpost or command center. From that place, they try to influence the surrounding region. God did the same by promising a land to Abraham, because He is the King.

When the British came to India, they didn't come in with an army to fight the rulers there. They came and established an outpost for their business. They acquired a piece of land from one of the kings in India. The rest is history. This is how kingdoms operate.

When the church goes into a new region, they put up a tent and conduct a crusade or hand out free meals. That's what non-profit or religious organizations do. That's not the way kingdoms operate. That's why we have almost no influence in any nation. The church is supposed to operate like a kingdom—like God has done throughout His written Word. God never instructed Abraham or anyone else to feed the hungry first when you go into a land. No.

The land God promised Abraham stretched from Egypt to Iraq. He also said every land Abraham would walk upon would belong to him. He told Joshua the same thing (Joshua 1:3). This is a promise we can practice as well.

The second thing God promised Abraham is a seed. Why a seed? Because every kingdom needs people to be sustained and grow. The strength of a king is in the multitude of his people (Proverbs 14:28). Also, a king who doesn't have a successor to continue his throne is considered cursed.

God promised Abraham that his descendants would be like the sand of the sea and the stars in the sky. Abraham lived like a king, even though he was not officially anointed to be a king like the other kings in the Old Testament. All these temporary rulers and kings were supposed to foreshadow the literal kingdom of the Messiah that Jesus would set up one day on this earth. Most of them failed in their assignment.

Moses

God used Moses to fulfill the promise He gave to Abraham. He used him to establish a nation and a royal priesthood. Studying the life of Moses is a good way to learn how to establish a nation. That is the principle we are supposed to learn from his life. Instead, we get stuck with the rules and regulations of Mosaic Law, and argue about them.

Moses established the economic, agricultural, educational, and judicial systems; moral and civil laws; the priesthood; and the basic fabric of family life: Through him, God established the very essence of the nation itself.

David

After Abraham, the next person God chose to play a major role in establishing His kingdom was David. Jesus is called the Son of David many times in the Gospels. As I mentioned earlier, the New Testament begins with this statement:

> The book of the genealogy of Jesus Christ, the Son of David, the Son of Abraham (Matthew 1:1).

David was the first person in the entire Bible who had a revelation of God as King and understood His kingdom. Though God wanted to be known as the King from the very beginning, it was hidden from mankind because of the enemy's deception.

Why does David play such a major role in God's kingdom in relation with Jesus Christ? Why is Jesus called "the Son of David" and not the Son of Moses or Elijah? If Abraham is the father of our faith, David is the father of the kingdom message.

If you read what David wrote about God in Psalms and other books, you will understand what I am talking about. David honored God as a King. He was more focused on that aspect of God's nature than any other. He was so passionate about God's kingdom that God made an unconditional and eternal covenant with him about David's throne and the generations after him.

As mentioned before, God always wanted to be the Ruler and the King of the earth. Because of the fall, people did not understand this anymore.

It became hidden from them by the deception of the enemy. Instead, the enemy had usurped God's place and appointed himself as the ruler of this world.

Satan wanted to be worshiped as a god. He did that directly and indirectly through idol worship. For example, the demonic god Molech (or Moloch in some versions) in the Old Testament actually means *king or ruler*. People of that time were serving this demon as their king. Baal, one of the other demonic entities that people were worshipping meant *master*. God wanted to be their Master and King, but they did not recognize it. They thought God was some power that would destroy everything or anything that disobeyed Him.

Until the time of David, the revelation of God as King was hidden from people. God found a man in David who was willing to bring that truth into the light. Do you think God was happy about that? You bet! That is why God said that David was a man after His own heart. God has the heart of a king, and David had a heart of a king too.

We have misinterpreted this for a long time, thinking God said that about David because of his singing and musical gift. This is not the case.

> Give heed to the voice of my cry, my King and my God, for to You I will pray (Psalm 5:2).

> The Lord is King forever and ever; the nations have perished out of His land (Psalm 10:16).

> For the kingdom is the Lord's, and He rules over the nations (Psalm 22:28).

Using a concordance, take the time to discover all the verses in which David talks about God as a King and His kingdom in Psalms, and you will see what I am talking about. Here's a secret too, and it is the best secret I have shared so far. Do you want God's favor and attention in your life? Then *treat and honor God like you treat and honor a King, and show interest in His kingdom.* You and your generations after you will never perish. God will begin to show personal interest on your behalf and your children.

God loves everyone. He used many people in the Bible, but not very many have the honor of being called Son of David, or the son of Abraham. Only two people in the entire history of the human race have such an honor. There are specific reasons for this. Many people relate David only with his singing and music. They jump and dance all day long and get nothing from God.

Why do I say that? Because I could not find one reference of a time when God did anything for David because of his singing, or a time when God commended David for his musical ability. If you know of a reference where He does, please let me know. The verse people normally go to is when God said David was the man after His own heart, but God was not referring to singing there. He was talking about having the heart of a king, because God is a King and has the heart of a king.

To God, David was not a musician, although he was talented musically and wrote many songs. To God, David was a king who ruled the nations as He would have ruled them Himself. That is why God was excited about David. He was looking for someone who would exercise His kingdom, dominion, and principle.

God blessed David in every way and made his name great like the great men on the earth. David subdued the earth and all his enemies under his feet (1 Chronicles 22:18). Only in David's time did this ever happen in the history of Israel, or the world, after the fall. The whole kingdom was established, and reached the zenith of its power, glory, and prosperity. The only time it will be any better is when Jesus rules on the earth in the millennium.

The only other person with whom God made an unconditional covenant was Abraham. When God called him, He did not mention any conditions. The only thing Abraham had to do was to obey whatever God told him to do. It was the same with David too. When God gave His promises, He did not say, "If you do this, then I will do that!" No, He did not speak thus to the people of Israel.

Though I could write much more about David and his life, I want to look at the covenant God made with him so that we understand the aspect of the kingdom of God that was revealed through his life. Through David, God established an eternal kingdom, an eternal throne, and an eternal dynasty. We read about the Davidic covenant in 2 Samuel:

> Go and tell My servant David, 'Thus says the Lord: "Would you build a house for Me to dwell in? For I have not dwelt in a house since the time that I brought the children of Israel up from Egypt, even to this day, but have moved about in a tent and in a tabernacle. Wherever I have moved about with all the children of Israel, have I ever spoken a word to anyone from the tribes of Israel, whom I commanded to shepherd My people Israel, saying, "Why have you not built Me a house of cedar?"" Now therefore, thus shall you say to My servant David, 'Thus says the Lord of hosts: "I took you from the sheepfold, from following the sheep, to be ruler over My people, over Israel. And I have been with you wherever you have gone, and have cut off all your enemies from before you, and have made you a great name, like the name of the great men who are on the earth. Moreover I will appoint a place for My people Israel, and will plant them, that they may dwell in a place of their own and move no more; nor shall the sons of wickedness oppress them anymore, as previously, since the time that I commanded judges to be over My people Israel, and have caused you to rest from all your enemies. Also the Lord tells you that He will make you a house.

> "When your days are fulfilled and you rest with your fathers, I will set up your seed after you, who will come from your body, and I will establish his kingdom. He shall build a house for My name, and I will establish the throne of his kingdom forever. I will be his Father, and he shall be My son. If he commits iniquity, I will chasten him with the rod of men and with the blows of the sons of men. But My mercy shall not depart from him, as I took it from Saul, whom I removed from before you. And your house and your kingdom shall be established forever before you. Your throne shall be established forever'" (2 Samuel 7:5-16).

The important part of that covenant is the second part in which God speaks about the kingdom and the throne. There is a double meaning to it because it is a prophecy about David's own immediate son and also of Jesus Christ, who would come thousands of years later through David's lineage. This is why Jesus is called the Son of David. Naturally speaking, Jesus came through David's bloodline. We can read more details about this covenant and its reference to Jesus in Psalm 89.

The Throne of God and Jesus Christ the King

God established the throne of David as an eternal throne—one upon which Jesus Christ will sit and rule the nations. The question is: When will this begin? We find the answer to that question in the following verses. When the angel of the Lord appeared to Mary to announce the birth of Jesus, he said this to her about the throne of David:

> "For unto us a Child is born, unto us a Son is given; and the government will be upon His shoulder…Of the increase of His government and peace there will be no end. Upon the throne of David and over His kingdom, to order it and establish it with judgment and justice from that time forward, even forever" (Isaiah 9:6a & 7).

And behold, you will conceive in your womb and bring forth a Son, and shall call His name Jesus. He will be great, and will be called the Son of the Highest; and the Lord God will give Him the throne of His father David. And He will reign over the house of Jacob forever, and of His kingdom there will be no end (Luke 1:31-33).

God is talking about David, his throne, and his kingdom. So, if Jesus came to sit on David's throne, why didn't He set up a physical throne in Jerusalem and rule Israel at His first coming? Jesus was born a king (Matthew 2:2). He did not have to wait until He was a certain age to become king like others do. He was their King while He was with them, even when He was just a baby. They did not recognize Him because He didn't have a palace or a throne. Even so He was very much a King in all respects. He is an eternal King and His kingdom has no end.

If you really look at the covenant God made with David, there is no mention of heaven or what David's children will be doing after they die. In the above prophecy of 2 Samuel 7 in verse 12 God said, "When your days are fulfilled and you rest with your fathers…" Notice the word "rest" and this is God speaking. That's what people do when they get to heaven, they rest until they can return to earth again. I hope you believe that God knows a little better about things than we do. The entire covenant God made with David has to do with the earth and the operation of God's kingdom here. The same thing can be seen in the covenant He made with Abraham.

For a long time I did not understand the message Peter preached on the day of Pentecost. I wondered why he didn't mention anything about the kingdom of God. Why was it only about repentance and baptism? I was ignorant and blinded by the religious spirit for a long time and that is why I did not see anything about God's kingdom in that message. Peter spoke about repentance and baptism only after people asked him what they should do—after they heard his preaching. The entire message Peter preached prior to that was about David and his throne, and how God raised Jesus to sit on that throne. *He preached the kingdom of God from a historical perspective, showing how Jesus had fulfilled the prophecies and promises God had given David about his throne.*

Peter preached more about the kingdom of God in that one message than anyone else in the entire book of Acts. He referred to David and his throne several times. What does David have to do with the day of Pentecost, or the arrival of the Holy Spirit, or the inauguration of the church? Why would Peter refer to David in the first message ever preached in the church age? This gets very interesting. There are ten references to David and nine references to Abraham in the book of Acts.

Throughout the Gospels, Jesus is called the Son of David. The Holy Spirit gave Peter a revelation about that when He stood up to preach. It had everything to do with God's eternal kingdom.

When those Jewish people heard that message, they were cut to the heart and ran to him. Jesus said that from the day of John the Baptist, the kingdom of God was being preached and everyone was pressing into it. Three thousand people ran to Peter to get into the kingdom that day.

> "Men and brethren, let me speak freely to you of the patriarch David, that he is both dead and buried, and his tomb is with us to this day. Therefore, being a prophet, and knowing that God had sworn with an oath to him that of the fruit of his body, according to the flesh, He would raise up the Christ to sit on his throne, he, foreseeing this, spoke concerning the resurrection of the Christ, that His soul was not left in Hades, nor did His flesh see corruption. This Jesus God has raised up, of which we are all witnesses. Therefore being exalted to the right hand of God, and having received from the Father

the promise of the Holy Spirit, He poured out this which you now see and hear.

"For David did not ascend into the heavens, but he says himself: 'The Lord said to my Lord, "Sit at My right hand, till I make Your enemies Your footstool"' (Acts 2:29-35).

It is interesting to look at how each of the Gospels presents the entry of Jesus into Jerusalem too. When the people shouted, "Hosanna in the highest" or "hosanna to the Son of David," Mark recorded it with David's kingdom, which we do not see in the other Gospels.

Then those who went before and those who followed cried out, saying: "Hosanna! Blessed is He who comes in the name of the Lord! Blessed is the kingdom of our father David that comes in the name of the Lord! Hosanna in the highest!" (Mark 11:9-10).

In His triumphal or royal entry into Jerusalem, He was also fulfilling one of the major prophecies in the Old Testament because He actually was their King.

Rejoice greatly, O daughter of Zion! Shout, O daughter of Jerusalem! Behold, your King is coming to you; He is just and having salvation, lowly and riding on a donkey, a colt, the foal of a donkey (Zechariah 9:9).

Thus we see that the kingdom of God was very much alive and was the focus of the lives of the Patriarchs.

Chapter 6
Dimension 4: Kingdom of God through the Nation of Israel

Chapter 6

Dimension 4: Kingdom of God through the Nation of Israel

When God established the nation of Israel as the beacon of hope for the whole world, He wanted them to be a kingdom of priests.

"And you shall be to Me a *kingdom* of priests and a holy nation." These are the words which you shall speak to the children of Israel (Exodus 19:6).

And your house and your *kingdom* shall be established forever before you. Your throne shall be established forever" (2 Samuel 7:16).

And of all my sons (for the Lord has given me many sons) He has chosen my son Solomon to sit on the throne of *the kingdom of the Lord* over Israel (1 Chronicles 28:5).

Yours, O Lord, is the greatness, the power and the glory, the victory and the majesty; for all that is in heaven and in earth is

Yours; *Yours is* the kingdom, O Lord, and You are exalted as head over all (1 Chronicles 29:11).

Then Solomon sat on the throne of the Lord *as king* instead of David his father, and prospered; and all Israel obeyed him (1 Chronicles 29:23).

The nation of Israel rejected God and His kingdom assignment for them. He allowed them to be taken captive, and they lost their homeland; but because of the covenant and promise He made with Abraham and David, the fulfillment of those promises has to come through the Jewish race. Jesus was born according to the scriptures as the son of David and He was sent to the nation of Israel.

This time they rejected Jesus as well. Not only did they reject Him, they crucified Him. So Jesus told them that the kingdom of God would be taken from them and given to a nation that will bear its fruit (Matthew 21:43). He also said many would come from the four corners of the earth and sit in His kingdom with Abraham, Isaac, and Jacob (Matthew 8:11).

At His first coming, Jesus was sent only to the nation of Israel. God wanted to give them the opportunity to accept His offer, but they rejected it. Jesus shared a parable about this to the Jewish leaders of His time, and they were not happy to hear it.

Parable about the People of Israel

Hear another parable: There was a certain landowner who planted a vineyard and set a hedge around it, dug a winepress in it and built a tower. And he leased it to vinedressers and went into a far country. Now when vintage-time drew near, he sent his servants to the vinedressers, that they might receive its fruit. And the vinedressers took his servants, beat one, killed one, and stoned another. Again he sent other servants, more than the first, and they did likewise to them. Then last of all he sent his son to them, saying, "They will respect my son." But when the vinedressers saw the son, they said among themselves, "This is the heir. Come, let us kill him and seize his inheritance." So they took him and cast him out of the vineyard and killed him. Therefore, when the owner of the vineyard comes, what will he do to those vinedressers?"

They said to Him, "He will destroy those wicked men miserably, and lease his vineyard to other vinedressers who will render to him the fruits in their seasons."

Jesus said to them, "Have you never read in the Scriptures: 'The stone which the builders rejected has become the chief cornerstone. This was the Lord's doing, and it is marvelous in our eyes'? Therefore I say to you, the kingdom of God will be taken from you and given to a nation bearing the fruits of it. And whoever falls on this stone will be broken; but on whomever it falls, it will grind him to powder."

Now when the chief priests and Pharisees heard His parables, they perceived that He was speaking of them. But when they sought to lay hands on Him, they feared the multitudes, because they took Him for a prophet (Matthew 21:33-46).

If we want to know how a kingdom is supposed to operate and how the church is supposed to function, we need to look at the nation of Israel. The way they lived and functioned should be our example. Their economy and government, as well as their judicial and educational systems are still the same; and the church should follow them. We do not need to follow the ceremonial laws or rituals, only the kingdom principles.

As I mentioned earlier, Israel was a nation; the church is called a nation as well. We are called an *ekklesia* and they were called an *ekklesia* too

(Matthew 16:18; Acts 7:38; 1 Peter 2:9). Based on what God told both of them, it is easy to make a comparison between them. You will be surprised to see that He told both of them the exact same things.

I am going to tell you something revolutionary. What the nation of Israel was in the Old Testament and is today, their blessings, technology, agriculture and productivity, the church needs to be in every nation on earth. That is how we should function as light and salt of the world and the earth.

Both Israel and the church have the same function and purpose. Whatever God told Israel, He also told the church. Here are a few examples:

When God called Abraham, He promised him that He would bless all the nations of the earth through him (Genesis 22:18). When Jesus told the church to go and disciple all nations, He used a different phrase, but it carried the same meaning (Matthew 28:19). You cannot disciple a nation without being a blessing to them.

God promised Abraham that his descendants would possess the gates of their enemies (Genesis 22:17). Jesus said He would build his church and the gates of hell would not prevail against it (Matthew 16:18).

The Israelites were called the children of God (Exodus 4:22; Deuteronomy 14:1). Anyone who believes in Jesus Christ is a child of God too (John 1:12).

God wanted them to be the head and above every other nation (Deuteronomy 28:13). We are called the light of this world and the salt of the earth (Matthew 5:13-14).

God wanted them to be a kingdom of priests and a holy nation (Exodus 19:6). Likewise, the church is called a royal priesthood and a holy nation (1 Peter 2:9).

God named Jacob, his children, and the nation, Israel (Exodus 19:6). The church is called the Israel of God (Galatians 6:16).

God used twelve men (sons of Jacob) to establish the nation of Israel (see Genesis 46:8-26). Jesus used twelve apostles as the foundation of His church (Ephesians 2:20).

God wanted Israel to make it known that He was their God to the ends of the earth (Joshua 4:23-24; Psalm 59:13; 98:3). Jesus told the church to go to the ends of the earth too (Acts 1:8).

God promised the land of Canaan to the people of Israel (Genesis 15:18). He also promised and gave the jurisdiction of the entire earth to the church (Matthew 5:5; Matthew 16:19).

Israel is called a nation (Genesis 19:6), and so is the church (Matthew 21:43; 1 Peter 2:9).

They were called the church, or congregation, in the wilderness (Exodus 12:3). We are the church in the New Testament (Acts 7:38, KJV; Acts 9:31).

All of the inhabitants of the land were afraid and became fainthearted because of the Israelites (Exodus 23:27; Joshua 2:10). Fear came upon every soul because of the church and what the Lord did through them (Acts 2:43).

God told Moses to appoint judges and officers throughout all the land to administer justice to the people (Deuteronomy 16:18). Jesus and Paul told us to do the same in the church (Matthew 18:15-17; Acts 14:23; 1 Corinthians 6:1-5; Titus 1:5).

Don't ever let anyone convince you that God didn't bless you with the same blessing He blessed the Jews.

- You are a child of God (John 1:12).

- You are a seed of Abraham (Galatians 3:29).

- You are a chosen generation (1 Peter 2:9).

- You received the promise of Abraham (Galatians 3:14).

- You are a coheir with Christ (Romans 8:17).

- You are grafted into the same blessings and promises God gave to the Jews.

Actually, you and I have received a better covenant than the Old Testament covenant! This is not replacement theology; this is called extended theology or oneness theology. God decided to *extend* the same blessings, promises, favor, protection, and prosperity He had bestowed on the Jews to the Gentiles through Jesus Christ, and create "one new man" (Ephesians 2:14-22) out of both. From the beginning, His plan was to have one family with Jesus as its Head: "one Lord, one faith, one baptism" (Ephesians 4:5).

As a Gentile, don't ever let anyone deceive you by saying you have to take part in Jewish rituals to receive a special blessing from your own Father. You do not. We can appreciate what God did for the Jewish people, but their practices will not give us a special blessing or a greater anointing. Conversely, we should never resent those who are Jewish; instead, we need to pray for the peace of Jerusalem and for the salvation of the Jewish people. They have the same opportunity to know Messiah that we do, and the same need.

Chapter 7
Dimension 5: Kingdom of God that came with the first coming of Jesus Christ

Chapter 7

Dimension 5: Kingdom of God that came with the first coming of Jesus Christ

From that time Jesus began to preach and to say, "Repent, for the kingdom of heaven is at hand" (Matthew 4:17).

When Jesus was on the earth, the kingdom manifested only where He was physically present. He showed the people what life in the kingdom should look like: He cast out demons because demons belong to another kingdom. He healed the sick and fed the hungry because there is no sickness or hunger in His kingdom.

Jesus revealed the culture of the kingdom. Everything He taught and each parable He shared was about one of the twelve components of His kingdom. Everything He taught revealed a mystery of the kingdom.

If we are supposed to seek the kingdom first, and the church is here to administer the kingdom of God, then we need to know what comprises that kingdom. A kingdom is made of twelve different components: 1) King, 2) Government/*Ekklesia*, 3) Territory, 4) Family, 5) Culture, 6) Decrees and Laws, 7) Army, 8) Education/

Teachings, 9) Economy/Treasury, 10) Business/Industry, 11) Media, and 12) Agriculture.

Below is a list of some of the parables and their connection to one of the twelve components of the kingdom. As you research these and discover the depth of His Word, you will find even more on your own during your personal study.

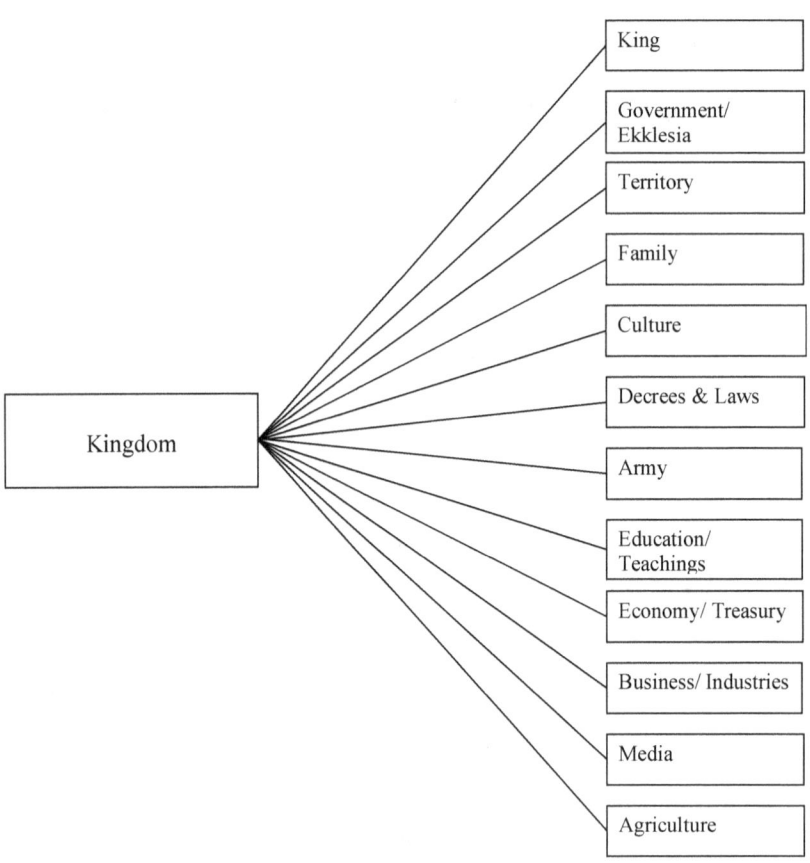

The King

- Parable of the king and his servants in Matthew 18:23-35.
- Parable of the king and the marriage feast in Matthew 22:1-14.

Territory/Land

- Parable of the landowner and hired servants in Matthew 20:1-16.
- Parable of the landowner and the vineyard in Matthew 21:33-46.

Culture

- Parable of the Good Samaritan in Luke 10:25-37.
- Parable of the friends at midnight in Luke 11:1-10.
- Parable of the birds and lilies in Matthew 6:25-34.

Government

- Parable of the rock and keys in Matthew 16:15-19.
- Parable of the unrighteous judge in Luke 18:1-8.

Decrees and Laws

Every parable in the Gospels contains decrees and laws of the kingdom of God. They are in every one.

Family

- Parable of the perfect father in Luke 15:11-32.
- Parable of the two sons and the vineyard in Matthew 21:28-32.
- Parable of the marriage feast and wedding garment in Matthew 22:1-14.

Economy

- Parable of the treasure and the field in Matthew 13:44.
- Parable of the talents and rewards in Matthew 25:14-30.
- Parable of the faithful steward in Luke 16:1-13.

Education

- Parable of the scribe and the householder in Matthew 13:51-52.
- All of Jesus' teachings are examples of kingdom education. He modeled how to teach and what was most important.

Army

- Parable of the king going to war in Luke 14:31-32.

Business and Industries

- Parable of the merchant and the pearl in Matthew 13:45-46.
- Parable of the faithful and wise servant in Matthew 24:45-51.
- Parable of the ten virgins in Matthew 25:1-13.
- Parable of the tower builder in Luke 14:25-30.
- Parable of the unrighteous steward in Luke 16:1-13.
- Parable of the nobleman and his ten servants in Luke 19:11-17.

Media

There is no need of any specific reference to media because whatever Jesus preached and taught was through the medium of speech and what others wrote. Both continue today.

Agriculture

There are more parables connected to agriculture and economy than any of the other areas. I believe this is because those two areas were connected to the lives of the people of that day more closely than others. They are also part of the foundation of kingdom economy.

- Parable of the sower and the seed in Matthew 13:3-23.
- Parable of the mustard tree and the birds in Matthew 13:31-32.
- Parable of the leaven and meal in Matthew 13:33-35.
- Parable of the good and bad fish in Matthew 13:47-50.
- Parable of the sheep and goats in Matthew 25:31-46.

How do we administer the kingdom of God so we can see nations being restored to God? As you read, I pray that this revelation will be deposited into your spirit and take root in your life, so that you will be able to discover which area you are called to influence and see your part in restoring your nation.

Chapter 8
Kingdom of God in the Four Gospels

Chapter 8

Kingdom of God in the Four Gospels

When Jesus spoke about the kingdom of heaven or God, He looked at it in seven different dimensions. God does not live in the confines of time, and everything Jesus said was the Word of God. Though He was human, He was fully God as well. Because we live in time, we really need to discern the time frame in Jesus' teaching.

Jesus went from past to present to future in the same chapter or even verse as He spoke in the Bible. He would talk about something that happened in the past, followed by something that was currently going on, and then touch on things that would happen in the millennium, all in the same verse. It can really cause confusion to a reader if we fail to discern what He is talking about.

When Jesus taught about the kingdom, He spoke of the eternal kingdom, the kingdom we need to experience right now, and the kingdom that was to come.

And I say to you that many will come from east and west, and sit down with Abraham, Isaac, and Jacob in *the kingdom* of heaven (Matthew 8:11).

But the sons of the *kingdom* will be cast out into outer darkness. There will be weeping and gnashing of teeth (Matthew 8:12).

Below are the all the references to the kingdom of God or kingdom of heaven in the four Gospels. I have categorized them so you know which time frame or dimension they fit into.

Gospel of Matthew

Eternal

For Yours is the kingdom and the power and the glory forever. Amen (Matthew 6:13b).

Israel

But the sons of the kingdom will be cast out into outer darkness. There will be weeping and gnashing of teeth (Matthew 8:12).

Then Jesus went about all the cities and villages, teaching in their synagogues, preaching the gospel of the kingdom, and healing every sickness and every disease among the people (Matthew 9:35).

Therefore I say to you, the kingdom of God will be taken from you and given to a nation bearing the fruits of it (Matthew 21:43).

Time of Jesus

In those days John the Baptist came preaching in the wilderness of Judea, and saying, "Repent, for the kingdom of heaven is at hand!" (Matthew 3:1-2).

From that time Jesus began to preach and to say, "Repent, for the kingdom of heaven is at hand" (Matthew 4:17).

And Jesus went about all Galilee, teaching in their synagogues, preaching the gospel of the kingdom, and healing all kinds of sickness and all kinds of disease among the people (Matthew 4:23).

Blessed are the poor in spirit, for theirs is the kingdom of heaven (Matthew 5:3).

Blessed are those who are persecuted for righteousness' sake, for theirs is the kingdom of heaven (Matthew 5:10).

Then Jesus went about all the cities and villages, teaching in their synagogues, preaching the gospel of the kingdom, and healing every sickness and every disease among the people (Matthew 9:35).

And as you go, preach, saying, "The kingdom of heaven is at hand" (Matthew 10:7).

And from the days of John the Baptist until now the kingdom of heaven suffers violence, and the violent take it by force (Matthew 11:12).

But if I cast out demons by the Spirit of God, surely the kingdom of God has come upon you (Matthew 12:28).

Therefore I say to you, the kingdom of God will be taken from you and given to a nation bearing the fruits of it (Matthew 21:43).

But woe to you, scribes and Pharisees, hypocrites! For you shut up the kingdom of heaven against men; for you neither go in yourselves, nor do you allow those who are entering to go in (Matthew 23:13).

Church

For I say to you, that unless your righteousness exceeds the righteousness of the scribes and Pharisees, you will by no means enter the kingdom of heaven (Matthew 5:20).

Your kingdom come. Your will be done on earth as it is in heaven (Matthew 6:10).

But seek first the kingdom of God and His righteousness, and all these things shall be added to you (Matthew 6:33).

Not everyone who says to Me, "Lord, Lord," shall enter the kingdom of heaven, but he who does the will of My Father in heaven (Matthew 7:21).

Assuredly, I say to you, among those born of women there has not risen one greater than John the Baptist; but he who is least in the kingdom of heaven is greater than he (Matthew 11:11).

He answered and said to them, "Because it has been given to you to know the mysteries of the kingdom of heaven, but to them it has not been given" (Matthew 13:11).

When anyone hears the word of the kingdom, and does not understand it, then the wicked one comes and snatches away what was sown in his heart. This is he who received seed by the wayside (Matthew 13:19).

Another parable He put forth to them, saying: "The kingdom of heaven is like a man who sowed good seed in his field" (Mathew 13:24).

Another parable He put forth to them, saying: "The kingdom of heaven is like a mustard seed, which a man took and sowed in his field" (Matthew 13:31).

Another parable He spoke to them: "The kingdom of heaven is like leaven, which a woman took and hid in three measures of meal till it was all leavened" (Matthew 13:33).

The field is the world, the good seeds are the sons of the kingdom, but the tares are the sons of the wicked one (Matthew 13:38).

Again, the kingdom of heaven is like treasure hidden in a field, which a man found and hid; and for joy over it he goes and sells all that he has and buys that field (Matthew 13:44).

Again, the kingdom of heaven is like a merchant seeking beautiful pearls (Matthew 13:45).

Again, the kingdom of heaven is like a dragnet that was cast into the sea and gathered some of every kind (Matthew 13:47).

Then He said to them, "Therefore every scribe instructed concerning the kingdom of heaven is like a householder who brings out of his treasure things new and old" (Matthew 13:52).

And I will give you the keys of the kingdom of heaven, and whatever you bind on earth will be bound in heaven, and whatever you loose on earth will be loosed in heaven (Matthew 16:19).

Assuredly, I say to you, there are some standing here who shall not taste death till they see the Son of Man coming in His kingdom (Matthew 16:28).

At that time the disciples came to Jesus, saying, "Who then is greatest in the kingdom of heaven?" (Matthew 18:1).

Assuredly, I say to you, unless you are converted and become as little children, you will by no means enter the kingdom of heaven (Matthew 18:3).

Therefore whoever humbles himself as this little child is the greatest in the kingdom of heaven (Matthew 18:4).

For there are eunuchs who were born thus from *their* mother's womb, and there are eunuchs who were made eunuchs by men, and there are eunuchs who have made themselves eunuchs for the *kingdom* of heaven's sake. He who is able to accept it, let him accept it (Matthew 19:12).

But Jesus said, "Let the little children come to Me, and do not forbid them; for of such is the *kingdom* of heaven" (Matthew 19:14).

Then Jesus said to His disciples, "Assuredly, I say to you that it is hard for a rich man to enter the kingdom of heaven" (Matthew 19:23).

And again I say to you, it is easier for a camel to go through the eye of a needle than for a rich man to enter the kingdom of God (Matthew 19:24).

"Which of the two did the will of his father?" They said to Him, "The first." Jesus said to them, "Assuredly, I say to you that tax collectors and harlots enter the kingdom of God before you" (Matthew 21:31).

And this gospel of the kingdom will be preached in all the world as a witness to all the nations, and then the end will come (Matthew 24:14).

Then the kingdom of heaven shall be likened to ten virgins who took their lamps and went out to meet the bridegroom (Matthew 25:1).

For *the kingdom of heaven is* like a man traveling to a far country, who called his own servants and delivered his goods to them (Matthew 25:14).

But I say to you, I will not drink of this fruit of the vine from now on until that day when I drink it new with you in My Father's kingdom (Matthew 26:29).

Millennium and Beyond

Whoever therefore breaks one of the least of these commandments, and teaches men so, shall be called least in the kingdom of heaven; but whoever does and teaches them, he shall be called great in the kingdom of heaven (Matthew 5:19).

And I say to you that many will come from east and west, and sit down with Abraham, Isaac, and Jacob in the kingdom of heaven. But the sons of the kingdom will be cast out into outer darkness. There will be weeping and gnashing of teeth (Matthew 8:11-12).

The Son of Man will send out His angels, and they will gather out of His kingdom all things that offend, and those who practice lawlessness (Matthew 13:41).

Then the righteous will shine forth as the sun in the kingdom of their Father. He who has ears to hear, let him hear! (Matthew 13:43).

At that time the disciples came to Jesus, saying, "Who then is greatest in the kingdom of heaven?" (Matthew 18:1).

Therefore the kingdom of heaven is like a certain king who wanted to settle accounts with his servants (Matthew 18:23).

And He said to her, "What do you wish?" She said to Him, "Grant that these two sons of mine may sit, one on Your right hand and the other on the left, in Your kingdom" (Matthew 20:21).

The kingdom of heaven is like a certain king who arranged a marriage for his son" (Matthew 22:2).

Then the King will say to those on His right hand, 'Come, you blessed of My Father, inherit the kingdom prepared for you from the foundation of the world'" (Matthew 25:34).

Gospel of Mark

Eternal

No verses.

Garden of Eden

No verses.

Patriarchs

No verses.

Israel

No verses.

Time of Jesus

Now after John was put in prison, Jesus came to Galilee, preaching the gospel of the kingdom of God (Mark 1:14).

The time is fulfilled, and the kingdom of God is at hand. Repent, and believe in the gospel (Mark 1:15).

And He said, "The kingdom of God is as if a man should scatter seed on the ground" (Mark 4:26).

Then He said, "To what shall we liken the kingdom of God? Or with what parable shall we picture it?" (Mark 4:30).

Blessed is the kingdom of our father David that comes in the name of the Lord! Hosanna in the highest! (Mark 11:10).

Now when Jesus saw that he answered wisely, He said to him, "You are not far from the kingdom of God." But after that no one dared question Him (Mark 12:34).

Joseph of Arimathea, a prominent council member, who was himself waiting for the kingdom of God, coming and taking courage, went in to Pilate and asked for the body of Jesus (Mark 15:43).

Church

And He said to them, "To you it has been given to know the mystery of the kingdom of God; but to those who are outside, all things come in parables" (Mark 4:11).

And He said to them, "Assuredly, I say to you that there are some standing here who will not taste death till they see the kingdom of God present with power" (Mark 9:1).

And if your eye causes you to sin, pluck it out. It is better for you to enter the kingdom of God with one eye, rather than having two eyes, to be cast into hell fire (Matthew 9:47).

But when Jesus saw it, He was greatly displeased and said to them, "Let the little children come to Me, and do not forbid them; for of such is the kingdom of God" (Mark 10:14).

Assuredly, I say to you, whoever does not receive the kingdom of God as a little child will by no means enter it (Mark 10:15).

Then Jesus looked around and said to His disciples, "How hard it is for those who have riches to enter the kingdom of God!" (Mark 10:23).

And the disciples were astonished at His words. But Jesus answered again and said to them, "Children, how hard it is for those who trust in riches to enter the kingdom of God!" (Mark 10:24).

It is easier for a camel to go through the eye of a needle than for a rich man to enter the kingdom of God (Mark 10:25).

Assuredly, I say to you, I will no longer drink of the fruit of the vine until that day when I drink it new in the kingdom of God (Mark 14:25).

Millennium and Beyond

No verses.

Gospel of Luke

Eternal

And He will reign over the house of Jacob forever, and of His kingdom there will be no end (Luke 1:33).

Garden of Eden

No verses.

Patriarchs

No verses.

Israel

No verses.

Time of Jesus

He said to them, "I must preach the kingdom of God to the other cities also, because for this purpose I have been sent" (Luke 4:43).

Now it came to pass, afterward, that He went through every city and village, preaching and bringing the glad tidings of the kingdom of God. And the twelve were with Him (Luke 8:1).

He sent them to preach the kingdom of God and to heal the sick (Luke 9:2).

But when the multitudes knew it, they followed Him; and He received them and spoke to them about the kingdom of God, and healed those who had need of healing (Luke 9:11).

And heal the sick there, and say to them, "The kingdom of God has come near to you" (Luke 10:9).

The very dust of your city which clings to us we wipe off against you. Nevertheless know this, that the kingdom of God has come near you (Luke 10:11).

But if I cast out demons with the finger of God, surely the kingdom of God has come upon you (Luke 11:20).

Then He said, "What is the kingdom of God like? And to what shall I compare it?" (Luke 13:18).

And again He said, "To what shall I liken the kingdom of God?" (Luke 13:20).

The law and the prophets were until John. Since that time the kingdom of God has been preached, and everyone is pressing into it (Luke 16:16).

Now when He was asked by the Pharisees when the kingdom of God would come, He answered them and said, "The kingdom of God does not come with observation" (Luke 17:20).

Nor will they say, "See here!" or "See there!" For indeed, the kingdom of God is within you (Luke 17:21).

But Jesus called them to Him and said, "Let the little children come to Me, and do not forbid them; for of such is the kingdom of God" (Luke 18:16).

Now as they heard these things, He spoke another parable, because He was near Jerusalem and because they thought the kingdom of God would appear immediately (Luke 19:11).

For I say to you, I will no longer eat of it until it is fulfilled in the kingdom of God (Luke 22:16).

He had not consented to their decision and deed. He was from Arimathea, a city of the Jews, who himself was also waiting for the *kingdom* of God (Luke 23:51).

Church

Then He lifted up His eyes toward His disciples, and said: "Blessed are you poor, for yours is the kingdom of God" (Luke 6:20).

And He said, "To you it has been given to know the mysteries of the kingdom of God, but to the rest it is given in parables, that 'Seeing they may not see, and hearing they may not understand'" (Luke 8:10).

But I tell you truly, there are some standing here who shall not taste death till they see the kingdom of God (Luke 9:27).

Jesus said to him, "Let the dead bury their own dead, but you go and preach the kingdom of God" (Luke 9:60).

But Jesus said to him, "No one, having put his hand to the plow, and looking back, is fit for the kingdom of God" (Luke 9:62).

So He said to them, "When you pray, say: Our Father in heaven, hallowed be Your name. Your kingdom come. Your will be done on earth as it is in heaven" (Luke11:2).

But seek the kingdom of God, and all these things shall be added to you (Luke 12:31).

Do not fear, little flock, for it is your Father's good pleasure to give you the kingdom (Luke 12:32).

Now when one of those who sat at the table with Him heard these things, he said to Him, "Blessed is he who shall eat bread in the kingdom of God!" (Luke 14:15).

Assuredly, I say to you, whoever does not receive the kingdom of God as a little child will by no means enter it (Luke 18:17).

And when Jesus saw that he became very sorrowful, He said, "How hard it is for those who have riches to enter the kingdom of God!" (Luke 18:24).

For it is easier for a camel to go through the eye of a needle than for a rich man to enter the kingdom of God (Luke 18:25).

So He said to them, "Assuredly, I say to you, there is no one who has left house or parents or brothers or wife or children, for the sake of the kingdom of God, who shall not receive many times more in this present time, and in the age to come eternal life" (Luke 18:29-30).

Therefore He said: "A certain nobleman went into a far country to receive for himself a kingdom and to return" (Luke 19:12).

When they are already budding, you see and know for yourselves that summer is now near. So you also, when you see these things happening, know that the kingdom of God is near. Assuredly, I say to you, this generation will by no means pass away till all things take place (Luke 21:30-32).

For I say to you, I will not drink of the fruit of the vine until the kingdom of God comes (Luke 22:18).

And I bestow upon you a kingdom, just as My Father bestowed one upon Me (Luke 22:29).

Millennium and Beyond

For I say to you, among those born of women there is not a greater prophet than John the Baptist; but he who is least in the kingdom of God is greater than he (Luke 7:28).

There will be weeping and gnashing of teeth, when you see Abraham and Isaac and Jacob and all the prophets in the kingdom of God, and yourselves thrust out (Luke 13:28).

They will come from the east and the west, from the north and the south, and sit down in the kingdom of God (Luke 13:29).

And so it was that when he returned, having received the kingdom, he then commanded these servants, to whom he had given the money, to be called to him, that he might know how much every man had gained by trading (Luke 19:15).

So you also, when you see these things happening, know that the kingdom of God is near (Luke 21:31).

That you may eat and drink at My table in My kingdom, and sit on thrones judging the twelve tribes of Israel (Luke 22:30).

Then he said to Jesus, "Lord, remember me when You come into Your kingdom" (Luke 23:42).

Gospel of John

Eternal

Jesus answered, "My kingdom is not of this world. If My kingdom were of this world, My servants would fight, so that I should not be delivered to the Jews; but now My kingdom is not from here" (John 18:36).

Garden of Eden

No verses.

Patriarchs

No verses.

Israel

No verses.

Time of Jesus

No verses.

Church

Jesus answered and said to him, "Most assuredly, I say to you, unless one is born again, he cannot see the kingdom of God" John 3:3).

Jesus answered, "Most assuredly, I say to you, unless one is born of water and the Spirit, he cannot enter the kingdom of God" (John 3:5).

Millennium and Beyond

No verses.

Chapter 9
Dimension 6: Kingdom of God in the Church Age

Chapter 9

Dimension 6: Kingdom of God in the Church Age

I have heard people say that the apostles did not preach about the kingdom as much as Jesus because that message was only for the people who lived in Jesus' time and it was not meant for us. That is far from true. There is plenty of evidence in the book of Acts showing that they preached the kingdom of God.

Jesus preached the kingdom of God after His resurrection:

> To whom He also presented Himself alive after His suffering by many infallible proofs, being seen by them during forty days and speaking of the things pertaining to the kingdom of God (Acts 1:3).

We learned earlier that Peter preached the kingdom of God.

Philip preached the kingdom of God to the people of Samaria:

> But when they believed Philip as he preached the things concerning the kingdom of God and the name of Jesus Christ, both men and women were baptized (Acts 8:12).

Paul preached the kingdom of God and also about entering it:

> And he went into the synagogue and spoke boldly for three months, reasoning and persuading concerning the things of the kingdom of God (Acts 19:8).

> "And indeed, now I know that you all, among whom I have gone preaching the kingdom of God, will see my face no more" (Acts 20:25).

> So when they had appointed him a day, many came to him at his lodging, to whom he explained and solemnly testified of the kingdom of God, persuading them concerning Jesus from both the Law of Moses and the Prophets, from morning till evening (Acts 28:23).

> Then Paul dwelt two whole years in his own rented house, and received all who came to him, preaching the kingdom of God and teaching the things which concern the Lord Jesus Christ with all confidence, no one forbidding him (Acts 28:30-31).

> Strengthening the souls of the disciples, exhorting them to continue in the faith, and saying, "We must through many tribulations enter the kingdom of God" (Acts 14:22).

When there are that many references to the apostles preaching the kingdom of God, it is difficult to understand why some so-called theologians have a problem approving the message of the kingdom today. *From the beginning, the religious system and the religious spirit have opposed the message of the kingdom of God.* When you see someone who does not like the message of the kingdom, it is evidence that a religious spirit is operating in that person. When Jesus was here, the Gentiles and the sinners did not oppose Him or what He preached, but the religious leaders did. They did not like what He preached.

The reason we do not see many references to the kingdom in Paul's epistles is because almost all of them were written to address problems in the churches that were already established by Paul. Their purpose was to validate, defend, and support the ministry Paul was doing and the revelations he received. Not everyone was happy about Paul and his work or what the Lord was doing through him. Some of the churches he established even began to question his calling and his authority as an apostle, especially the church in Corinth.

Paul preached about many subjects, but he did not neglect the kingdom. He preached the cross, Christ crucified, grace, the second coming of Christ, about love and sin, and much more. It is almost impossible to list all the subjects he taught and illuminated for the body. When we read the epistles, we understand the depth of revelation he had on Christ, church, family, and everything that benefits a believer in Christ. All of these ideas are part of the kingdom; they are one package. That means that everything Paul preached was also about establishing and administering the kingdom of God. Its advancement was the focal point of his life's ministry.

There is a very different dimension of the kingdom of God operating now than when Jesus was physically on the earth. Otherwise He wouldn't have said some of the things He shared when He was here. If you remember when Jesus began His public ministry, He started by telling people to repent because the kingdom of God was very near or about to manifest. However, we do not hear anyone preaching such things after the day of Pentecost. That means something happened between Jesus' preaching in the Gospels and the arrival of the Holy Spirit.

> Assuredly, I say to you, there are some standing here who shall not taste death till they see the Son of Man coming in His kingdom (Matthew 16:28).

> And He said to them, "Assuredly, I say to you that there are some standing here who will not taste death till they see the kingdom of God present with power" (Mark 9:1).

During Jesus' time, the kingdom of God was limited only to where Jesus was physically located. When Jesus was walking on the earth, people in India, China, or other places could not experience what the people in Israel were experiencing.

When Jesus ascended after the resurrection, the kingdom of God left with Him. There was no one preaching or doing anything with the message of the kingdom, at least there is no evidence in the Bible that it was happening. Only 120 people were waiting and praying in an upper room. With the arrival of the Holy Spirit, the kingdom of God began to operate on earth in a new dimension.

This is the dimension of the kingdom that God has made available to each believer in this day and age. That is why Jesus told us to seek His kingdom first. Today we can receive the Holy Spirit within us to transform our hearts and direct our lives, like the people could not before Pentecost. God is now within us! We have particular missions to complete with His help and guidance in our lives.

If we only needed to know the things of the kingdom when we got to heaven, He did not have to tell us about them until later. Instead Jesus left ample instruction about His kingdom, so that when we had been endued with power from on high, we would be able to walk as He did and change our culture. Jesus did not waste His time teaching and preaching the kingdom of God during His earthly ministry. Jesus knew that the teaching He gave was what we would hear. He knew what was important and gave His kingdom top priority.

Jesus taught and asked His disciples to preach about the dimension of the kingdom that was about to come to this earth.

> And as you go, preach, saying, "The kingdom of heaven is at hand" (Matthew 10:7).

The kingdom has come upon us.

"But if I cast out demons by the Spirit of God, surely the kingdom of God has come upon you" (Matthew 12:28).

We are privileged to know the mysteries of His kingdom.

He answered and said to them, "Because it has been given to you to know the mysteries of the kingdom of heaven, but to them it has not been given" (Matthew 13:11).

We are supposed to enter the kingdom.

For I say to you, that unless your righteousness exceeds the righteousness of the scribes and Pharisees, you will by no means enter the kingdom of heaven (Matthew 5:20).

"Not everyone who says to Me, 'Lord, Lord,' shall enter the kingdom of heaven, but he who does the will of My Father in heaven" (Matthew 7:21).

Even the parables Jesus shared are three-dimensional. This means that He talked about the kingdom parable that was already happening, then He shared a parable that only related to the people of Israel, and then He shared a parable related to His kingdom that was going to happen at His second coming. The Word of God is so deep that there are always many facets and myriad applications to it. The Bible says, "The words of the Lord are pure words, like silver tried in a furnace of earth, purified seven times" (Psalm 12:6).

Chapter 10
The Book of Acts from a Kingdom Perspective

Chapter 10

The Book of Acts from a Kingdom Perspective

"He will subdue the peoples under us, and the nations under our feet"
(Psalm 47:3).

Acts begins and ends with the kingdom message (Acts 1:3; 28:30-31). The number twelve is the number of government in the Bible. In Acts 1 after Judas committed suicide, the eleven disciples came together to select a new disciple to replace him. They gathered in the upper room, and there were one hundred and twenty people waiting and praying. One hundred and twenty is ten times twelve. Then on the day of Pentecost, three thousand souls were saved after Peter preached the inaugural message of the church. Three thousand is two hundred and fifty times twelve. The twenty-four elders around the throne in heaven is twelve times two. Everything God does has a kingdom flavor.

Have you ever wondered how twelve men in the first century reached the entire known world in their lifetime with the gospel of the kingdom? More than one billion believers have been trying to do this for decades, and still half of the world remains unreached!

For three-and-a-half years, the main focus of Jesus' training and teaching to His disciples was the kingdom of God. Even after the resurrection, He talked with them about the kingdom for forty days. Jesus' priority is His kingdom: He wants to see the will of His Father accomplished.

Although the church would be the greatest enterprise God ever began, Jesus, the Head of the church, taught about it only twice in His entire recorded preaching and teaching. On the other hand, He mentioned His kingdom more than a hundred times in the four Gospels.

Jesus wanted His disciples to become familiar with how His kingdom operated. He wanted to create a kingdom mindset in them before they ever got to do anything with His church. He knew that without that, the church wouldn't be effective. *Only when we understand the kingdom can we clearly understand the purpose of the church.* The church is here to administer God's kingdom, but if its leaders don't know what the kingdom is and how it works, how can they administer it?

We cannot understand the doctrine of the church if we do not understand the doctrine of the kingdom of God first. This is the reason Jesus taught about the kingdom more than He taught about the church. He needed to establish the kingdom before He established the church—because the church is here to administer the kingdom. If there is no kingdom, then there is no need for a church.

We do not do that today. We teach about the church first and neglect the kingdom. The church has been functioning without the kingdom and it is powerless.

The Church: A Familiar Term

Some people think the concept of the church did not begin until His resurrection. That is not true. The church has been on the earth ever since kingdoms, or the kingdom of God, began to operate here. Every kingdom had an *ekklesia* that administered its policies and rules. Without an *ekklesia* (church), a kingdom cannot operate; and without a kingdom, a church will not survive.

The reason the disciples did not question Jesus about the church when He mentioned it was because they were familiar with the concept of kingdoms having an *ekklesia* from a historic perspective (Israel was a kingdom), and from the political climate in which they were living (Rome occupied Judea at this time). They knew Jesus was a king and that every king needed an *ekklesia*.

As mentioned before, it was a political term used in the Greek world to represent a group of citizens who were called out from among the people by a king or a government to administer the political, judicial, economic, and social affairs of the kingdom for the people. It was never used to address a group of people who worshiped, preached, or sang.

Every king and kingdom had an *ekklesia* that governed its affairs. Jesus added a spiritual dimension to His kingdom and *ekklesia* when He said, "I will build my church" (Matthew 16:18), because His kingdom is a spiritual kingdom. Jesus is King, so He needs an *ekklesia* to govern the affairs of His kingdom. That is why He started the church.

Each time Jesus mentioned the church He referred to a governing body, not a place of worship. He referred to a group of people who were assigned to exercise authority to solve problems both in *the spiritual* and in *the natural* world. In the political world of those days, the *ekklesia* was a group of people who were called out—or selected—from the general public to govern the affairs of the nation.

The disciples knew that every king had an *ekklesia* in his kingdom that governed his affairs. That's why they kept asking Jesus when He was going to set up His kingdom on the earth. They wanted to sit and rule with Him (Matthew 20:21; Acts 1:6). In Matthew, we notice that it was after Jesus said He would build His *ekklesia* that the mother of James and John came with the request for her sons to sit on His right and on His left in His kingdom (Matthew 20:20-21). They wanted to be part of the governing body of His kingdom, but they only understood the natural aspect of the term. That's what they were familiar with at that time. The spiritual revelation of His kingdom or *ekklesia* came to them later.

Preparing for the Kingdom

Jesus wanted His disciples to have a kingdom perspective, a kingdom worldview. He wanted them to see the world through that kingdom paradigm before they got to do anything with the church. To prepare them, He taught them day and night. He trained them for three-and-a-half years about how the kingdom worked. By the time the church started, they had a kingdom mindset. That is why they were able to reach the whole known world with the gospel of the kingdom. Wherever they went and whatever they did, they did it according to a kingdom mindset, thus the church came out of the kingdom.

When we receive the kingdom as a whole and administer it effectively in our communities and nations, the change we are looking for will happen. If we train our children to do the same, the ground we gain will be retained for generations to come. That is God's heart, and that is the mandate of the kingdom.

The kingdom of God is an invisible kingdom. We cannot see how it operates with our natural eyes. He put His kingdom inside of us and it manifests to the world through the work we do. It is God's desire that His will is done *on this earth as it is in heaven*. Because the earth was entrusted to us from the beginning, this can only be done through human beings. The new era of the kingdom of God began to operate with the coming of the Holy Spirit on the day of Pentecost. The *ekklesia* of Jesus' kingdom began to operate from that day. We do not see anyone preaching that the kingdom is at hand after the day of Pentecost because by then it was in full operation. The kingdom brought restoration.

Today we must approach church with a kingdom mindset too. Before the *ekklesia* can operate properly, there has to be a kingdom in place. If there is no kingdom, we do not need an *ekklesia* to govern it. Jesus established the kingdom first, and the ekklesia was founded on it. We have left that base. The problem today is there are many so-called *ekklesias* out there operating without proper knowledge of the kingdom. The sad result is that we are not effective.

Now let's see how the kingdom of God was administered through the early church and how each component of the kingdom played out through the book of Acts.

1: The King

The first and most important component of a kingdom is the king. Jesus promised us that where two or three are gathered in His name, He will be there in their midst (Matthew 18:20). He also promised His disciples that though He would be taken away from them for a little while, He would come back to them (John 16:16-17). In Acts, God is referred to as the Holy Spirit and sometimes as Jesus because the Father, Son, and the Holy Spirit are all one. The concept of the Trinity is there even though the word is not used.

2: The Government

The second component is the government. The church is the governing body of the kingdom of God. Acts gives many examples on how the apostles governed in the first century. The early church operated as a kingdom.

3: Territory

The third component of a kingdom is territory. Before Jesus ascended to heaven He commissioned the disciples and told them the span of the territory to which He wanted them to spread His message. In Acts 1:8,

He told them that after the Holy Spirit came upon them, they would be His witnesses in Jerusalem, Judea, Samaria, and to the ends of the earth. When the Holy Spirit came, there were people from every nation under heaven in Jerusalem to witness it (Acts 2:5).

They went from town to town, city to city, and nation to nation, preaching the gospel of the kingdom and overthrowing the kingdom (and the powers) of darkness, thereby establishing the will of their King.

4: Family

The fourth component of a kingdom is family, or people. There were a hundred and twenty people, both men and women, including husbands and wives, in the upper room when the Holy Spirit came. On the Day of Pentecost, three thousand souls were saved and the *ekklesia* officially began to function. As the church grew, God's message of salvation, deliverance, love, and grace was preached. "Family" was a basic theme in their words and writings from the beginning. Paul especially gave detailed instruction about how the body should interact as well as how we should treat one another in our families.

5: Culture

The fifth component of a kingdom is culture. Those who became part of the *ekklesia* had a different culture than the other citizens of the country. Righteousness, love, peace, and joy in the Holy Spirit was their culture. They shared everything in common. They had a different culture than the people outside of the church. They had a different "taste" than those around them; we should retain that difference today as well.

6: Decrees and Laws

The sixth component of a kingdom is the decrees and laws of the king. When the Holy Spirit came, it was Peter who began to proclaim, under the power of the Holy Spirit, the words Jesus put in his heart to speak. He was not waiting there with a prepared message with notes and references. He had no idea what he was going to say, nor did he know he would be preaching that day. Those were the decrees and laws the King announced to the public.

When the church began, they functioned under the doctrine of the apostles, the decrees and laws of the kingdom. Whatever the King wanted to communicate, He communicated through the apostles, His ambassadors. When they sent a message to another group of believers, the message was called a decree. Only kings and kingdoms issue decrees.

> "And as they went through the cities, they delivered to them the decrees to keep, which were determined by the apostles and elders at Jerusalem" (Acts 16:4).

7: The Army

The seventh component of a kingdom is the army. Every believer was a soldier, and the apostles were like generals in the army. This was a different kind of army, and they did not fight with swords and spears, but they had authority over all other kingdoms and kings in the natural and in the spirit. Many times when the apostles were arrested and put in prison by the rulers of a natural kingdom, the *ekklesia* prayed and cancelled the rule and authority of those kingdoms and governments (Acts 5:17-20; 12:3-11; 16:20-26).

8: Education and Teaching

The eighth component of a kingdom is education. Jesus commanded them to go into all the world and teach all nations everything He taught them (Matthew 28:20). In Acts, we read the teachings of the apostles. The epistles are full of teaching and training from Paul, Peter, John, and others for the *ekklesia*.

9: The Economy or Treasury

The ninth component of a kingdom is its economy, or treasury. There was not a single believer in the early church who was in want. No one had a need that was not met. I find this extremely interesting because we, on the other hand, spend so much time making money just to survive. How did that happen? What kind of financial system did they use? They established a kingdom economy to meet the needs of every single member in the church.

They set up a *kingdom banking* system to meet the needs of the church. At first when I read about it, I thought it was a *welfare system* to help the poor; but later, when the Holy Spirit opened my eyes to the kingdom, I understood that it was a banking system. A kingdom's wealth is a literal commonwealth, meaning that all the wealth is available to everyone. This is not the same meaning[3] used today in nations that call themselves commonwealths. They do not function as the church did.

I used to think that when the church began in Acts 2, everybody sold everything they had and brought the money to the apostles and they all waited around in the temple for Jesus to come back. That is not what happened either. Most of them only sold a portion of their possessions, house, or land, and brought it to the apostles. Then the apostles distributed it as need arose, and there was no one in the early church who was in need. That is kingdom living.

> "Now the multitude of those who believed were of one heart and one soul; neither did anyone say that any of the things he possessed was his own, but they had all things in common. And with great power the apostles gave witness to the resurrection of the Lord Jesus. And great grace was upon them all.

---

3 "Commonwealth," Vocabulary.com, accessed February 15, 2017, https://www.vocabulary.com/dictionary/commonwealth.

> Nor was there anyone among them who lacked; for all who were possessors of lands or houses sold them, and brought the proceeds of the things that were sold, and laid them at the apostles' feet; and they distributed to each as anyone had need" (Acts 4:32-35).

If they had sold everything they had, they could not have met from house to house every day. The following verse says they sold possessions and goods, referring to real estate and products, and they met from house to house daily.

> "Now all who believed were together, and had all things in common, and sold their possessions and goods, and divided them among all, as anyone had need. So continuing daily with one accord in the temple, and breaking bread from house to house, they ate their food with gladness and simplicity of heart" (Acts 2:44-46).

> "And daily in the temple, and in every house, they did not cease teaching and preaching Jesus as the Christ" (Acts 5:42).

I believe that when each *ekklesia* reaches three thousand people (that's when it happened in the early church), they should start their own banking system. We should not depend on the world's economy world, but show the world how a kingdom economy operates.

On the day of Pentecost, three thousand souls were saved, and the New Testament church was born. Imagine an *ekklesia* with three thousand members at the present day. If they were all working to support their families, each of them would have income and a bank account. In the United States, the average person makes twenty thousand dollars a year (and many make much more than that), but for my purpose here,

I am imagining the least amount. If you multiply three thousand by twenty thousand, the total comes to sixty million dollars a year. Wow! It could be closer to a hundred million or even more because most people make significantly more than twenty thousand a year. That's the minimum amount of money that would come and go through that body in a year. That is a lot of money! And that's just one local church.

What if a church had a banking system to manage that much money instead of depending on a bank that is run by unbelievers using our money to support the kingdom of darkness and its agenda? *If you calculate all the money you make and the money you spend, you will see that most of your money goes back into the pockets of the ungodly.* The wicked become wealthier and wealthier, while the righteous come to church and cry out every day for a financial breakthrough. Lord, have mercy!

What if we had a system to keep our money within the kingdom of God? We need to use God's wisdom and knowledge to create and manage wealth. We need to study and practice kingdom economy. It is the church that makes the ungodly wealthy, but we do not recognize it. We have been blinded by the devil.

It will take wisdom and a lot of planning and trained individuals to do this, but it is possible. That's how it happened in the early church. Imagine that three thousand people sold part of their possessions, goods, houses, or land, and brought the money and put it at the feet of the apostles. How much money was it? Who managed all that money? What was the system they used to do it? A kingdom economy. In the early church, they did not borrow money from the world to buy a house or send their children to school. That is totally unacceptable in the kingdom of God.

It is important to note that they sold possessions and goods. To whom did they sell these? I am sure it was to the people in the church and outside the church. We need to encourage believers to come up with products that they can sell to generate income. That's the way we tap into the wealth of the wicked and create money for kingdom purposes.

If a particular kingdom citizen goes to a different kingdom to borrow money for their livelihood, to build a house, or for anything, who does that affect most? The king in that kingdom. It affects his reputation because it demonstrates the king's inability to meet the needs of his people. This is what we have been doing for a long time, but no more. In Acts and the epistles, believers (kingdom citizens) are not going out and borrowing money from unbelievers for anything.

The book of Acts should be our blueprint for running a church, because it operated like a kingdom. When one church had a financial struggle or was affected by famine, another church that was doing well sent help and support (Acts 11:28-29; 1 Corinthians 16:1-4; 2 Corinthians 9:1-5). This way their wealth always stayed in the church, and subsequently, in the kingdom. We have much to learn about kingdom economy. When the whole church is united, as Jesus wants it to be, we will be the largest economic force on the planet.

If the church in each nation was united, they would be the largest economic force in that nation. Then we could lend money to unbelievers and invest in different projects for the development of that nation. That money could be used to support the church and its ministries, instead of depending only on tithes and offerings. There would be no unmet needs in our churches, just like it was in the early church. That is what the Bible teaches. We should be lending and not borrowing because we represent and live in the most prosperous kingdom of all: God's.

The devil knows more about God, His kingdom, and how it operates than most Christians, including preachers, because he was with God and knew Him personally. I am currently working on a book about kingdom economy, which should be released sometime in 2018. The subtitle of that book is *Why All Tithe-Giving Believers Do Not Receive a Financial Breakthrough*. Make sure you get it and read it. I am asking you to spread the news about this kingdom message to your friends and family. People are tired of religion and rituals. They are looking for something real, something that works.

10: Media

The tenth component is the media. During the first century there was no electronic media like we use today. The only media available were preaching and writing. In the book of Acts, they were busy using both. We should utilize and maximize every form of media available to spread the gospel of the kingdom, using all our resources.

11: Business and Industry

The eleventh component of the kingdom is business and industry. As the church grew, believers began to do business, and people who were in business were added to the church. We read about prominent men and women who were won to Christ by the apostles. Many of them excelled in business and politics and were prosperous. Paul was a tentmaker. He supported his ministry team and personal life through that business.

Dorcas and Lydia were businesswomen too (Acts 9:39 and 16:14). Dorcas made robes and other clothing, while Lydia had a business in dying textiles. They both had products they sold. Many other believers also had trades and businesses. One of Paul's primary admonitions was to do good works. The phrase *good works* appears twenty-eight times in the New Testament. The Greek word for "work" is *ergon*, which means "to work, business, employment, that with which anyone is occupied. Any product whatever, anything accomplished by hand, art, industry, or mind."[4]

The Bible refers to our natural gift, trade, or occupation as our good works.

"For we are His workmanship, created in Christ Jesus for *good works*, which God prepared beforehand that we should walk in them" (Ephesians 2:10).

---

4 James Strong, "Strong's Greek: 2041, ἔργον (ergon) – work," Strong's Greek: 2041, ἔργον (ergon) – work, accessed February 15, 2017, http://biblehub.com/greek/2041.htm.

In the church, we have limited "good works" to things like helping orphans, feeding the poor, or visiting nursing homes and prisons, instead of its real and fuller meaning. *Anything* you do that is productive and fruitful is a good work. Any work that God gave you to do is a good work. That means that a mother caring for her children is doing a good work and is pleasing to God. Similarly, the person who works and develops his talents in any field is pleasing God. Jesus and Paul tell believers again and again to engage themselves in good works.

Jesus said people will glorify our heavenly Father is by seeing our good works. We, the children of God, are supposed to be the most productive people on earth!

> "Let your light so shine before men, that they may see your good works and glorify your Father in heaven" (Matthew 5:16).

The light Jesus refers to in this verse is our good works. He also said that we are the light of the world (Matthew 5:14). That means if anything good is going to happen, it has to come through us. The Lord told me a few years ago that He wanted to release every new invention through one of His children and His church, but that His children were all busy singing and waiting for a revival or the rapture. Therefore, He had to choose an unbeliever to release those ideas instead, and they are making billions of dollars with them.

12: Agriculture

The twelfth component of a kingdom is agriculture. We cannot live without food. The early church grew to thousands and thousands of people in the first few months. They fed all those people daily. Jesus, their King, taught them how to feed a multitude and how to manage big crowds.

In the Gospels when the people were hungry, Jesus told His disciples to feed them (Luke 9:19). Their idea was to collect some money and go to the next town and buy food to feed the five thousand men plus women and children. But that was not Jesus' plan. He has provision in His kingdom to feed the entire world each day. He taught them a very important lesson that day, one we all need to practice: Don't depend on the world for your food supply. Depend on His kingdom, and produce your own food. I do not believe Jesus did a miracle every day to feed everyone then or expected us to do that now, but He gives us ideas of how to produce our food and we can put those ideas to work.

In Acts believers used to meet in the temple and break bread from house to house daily. In Acts 6, a complaint about the fairness of the daily food distribution came up, so the apostles selected leaders to take care of the problem.

Influencing Earth with Heaven

When you read Acts with a kingdom mindset, you can see that all the aspects of the kingdom were active in the early church. They functioned as a kingdom would function and not as a religious or charitable organization. They were not a not-for-profit organization trying to feed the world. That was not their mission. They put into practice what Jesus had taught them. The Holy Spirit had empowered them to administer God's kingdom here. That's why they were able to reach the entire known world in their lifetime. Today, we are trying to reach the world with a church or religious mindset and are not that effective as a result.

The gospel of the kingdom affects every aspect of society. It is not focused on people getting to heaven. Jesus and His disciples never spoke with the goal of taking people to heaven anywhere in the Gospels or Acts. None of their messages ended by asking people, "How many of you want to receive Jesus and go to heaven? Please raise your hands." Nobody preached like that in the Bible.

There are people who are saved and attend churches worldwide, but are still hungry and broke. Their families and countries are in shambles.

What is the solution? The gospel of the kingdom. *They only heard the gospel of salvation.* Some evangelist went there and preached and they accepted Jesus, so they could go to heaven and they are waiting for Him to come and fetch them away.

What the Holy Spirit is sharing with you through this book are seeds of the kingdom. It's up to you to nurture, research, study, and pray to receive more revelation about each of these subjects. It's time for us to change the way we do church. Actually, it's almost too late to change. We need to tear down the religious strongholds and root the enemy out of our lives and begin again.

The focal point of the gospel of the kingdom is to influence earth with heaven. That is our primary goal. That is the main focus of the prayer Jesus taught us to pray, which most of us do not pray anymore. *We are to influence the culture of earth with the culture of heaven.*

Every nation has the twelve components I mentioned above, but they are not healthy and real; only the kingdom of God has the real stuff. When we administer the kingdom of God to the nations of the world, we will see them come to Christ one by one. As a result, Jesus will return.

Jesus said, "When this gospel of the kingdom shall be preached as a witness to all nations then the end will come" (Matthew 24:14). Jesus and His disciples preached the gospel of the kingdom. Which gospel are we preaching these days? Every denomination seems to have its own version. There is the Baptist gospel, Pentecostal gospel, Catholic gospel, and many others. When we preach the gospel of the kingdom, then the end will come.

Chapter 11
Dimension 7: Kingdom of God During the Millennial Reign and Beyond

Chapter 11

Dimension 7: Kingdom of God During the Millennial Reign and Beyond

The Son of Man will send out His angels, and they will gather out of His kingdom all things that offend, and those who practice lawlessness (Matthew 13:41).

Then the righteous will shine forth as the sun in the kingdom of their Father. He who has ears to hear, let him hear! (Matthew 13:43).

Then the King will say to those on His right hand, "Come, you blessed of My Father, inherit the kingdom prepared for you from the foundation of the world" (Matthew 25:34).

The earth will be restored to the way it was in the garden of Eden. This is the entire story and theme of the Bible. We are in that process and part of that restoration process.

> Whom heaven must receive until the times of restoration of all things, which God has spoken by the mouth of all His holy prophets since the world began (Acts 3:21).

Note that this verse says "restoration of *all* things" and not destruction of all things. Christians today are waiting for the destruction of all things. If something is destroyed, you cannot restore it; you have to recreate it. God is planning to "restore" the earth.

Next it says God has spoken about that restoration through *all* of His holy prophets since the world began. That means that every prophet that ever lived spoke the same thing. That is good news to me.

Jesus is coming back to reign on earth as the rightful King. All other kings and kingdoms must lay their crown and trophies at His feet. Every knee shall bow, and that includes the knees of every great king who ever lived and reigned, including David and the royal families of England and Europe.

Jesus will reign for a thousand years, basing His headquarters in Jerusalem. Then the final judgment will occur. After the millennial reign, Satan will be released for a short period of time. We will be tempted like Adam was tempted and we will need to overcome Satan this time. God will do this to give us an opportunity to have victory in the same area in which we failed in the book of Genesis.

The earth will be restored to how it was before the fall. There won't be any sickness, disease, curse, death, or tears. God's kingdom will be fully manifested, and we shall reign on the earth forever and ever—as God intended from the very beginning. What began in Genesis 1 will end at the same place in Revelation 22.

> There shall be no night there: They need no lamp nor light of the sun, for the Lord God gives them light. And they shall reign forever and ever (Revelation 22:5).

Chapter 12
The Present Kingdom

Chapter 12

The Present Kingdom

Jesus came to announce the imminent arrival of the kingdom. That was His primary mission, in addition to paying the penalty for our sin by His own blood. Once that was paid, there was reconciliation between God and man, and heaven and earth. God's kingdom could manifest once again on earth as it had in the beginning.

During the time of Jesus, the manifestation of the kingdom of God was limited to where He was physically present. When He went to Galilee from Jerusalem, the kingdom went with Him. Without Him, there was no kingdom manifestation.

After the Holy Spirit came, that was not the case anymore. The Holy Spirit is not limited to one place: He is omnipresent, which means He is present everywhere, all the time. Now the manifestation of the kingdom is not limited to any one place or time. The only limitation set today is how much mankind is willing to cooperate with God. God sent the Holy Spirit so His kingdom could be made manifest without any limitation of time or space.

We have been misinformed for too long about our mission on earth. The reason we win souls now is not just to take people to heaven, but to give them the opportunity to cooperate with God, to become part of God's team, and then manifest His kingdom on earth.

As we study the Gospels it is very important to understand the dimension of the kingdom that is operating on earth right now. There have been various schools of thought and many of them are twisted, formed from scriptures that are taken out of context.

Jesus taught us to pray for His kingdom to come and His will to be done on earth as it is in heaven: What does that mean exactly? What does that look like in this day and age? The church's primary mission is not to take over governments and nations by force or to bring them all under the reign of Jesus right now. Our primary focus is to influence our area, and accomplish God's will in every aspect of our society.

As a result, if a whole nation, city, or town turns to Jesus and become saved, praise God! We can really administer His kingdom in that place. Do I believe every nation on earth will come under the reign of Jesus before His second coming? The answer is no.

It is very important to understand the political background in Jesus' day when He was preaching the gospel of the kingdom to the Jews. They were under the oppression of Rome, and they were waiting for the deliverance and restoration of the nation of Israel. They believed that the Messiah would come, and that if He came, He would surely free them from their enemies and restore their nation.

Then Jesus appeared on the scene and began to preach about the kingdom of God. At first, most Jewish people were hesitant to believe in Him because He did not fit into their idea of a king or a deliverer. After seeing miracles and the way He fed five thousand people, they began to realize that He might be the Deliverer they were all waiting for.

They began to slowly put their trust in Him, expecting Him to be their king. After feeding the five thousand, they actually tried to make Him king (John 6:15), but He did not accept their offer. In truth, He was already their king, but a different kind of a King. Jesus did not come to give them political freedom because He knew that man's number one need was not for that. Man's number one need was spiritual. That is why in all politically free countries people still remain under bondage to spiritual oppression.

This is where the Jewish people, including the disciples, failed to understand Jesus' mission before His death, resurrection, and ascension. They did not understand spiritual freedom because they were spiritually blind. They only lens they saw freedom through was political: freedom from Roman rule. Jesus knew that no one became truly free just because they lived in a free society. He was more concerned about the internal freedom than the external. There are millions of people who live in free society today that are not free spiritually. They are bound and blind, and their condition is worse than my words can express.

Only after the arrival of the Holy Spirit on the day of Pentecost did the disciples understand the mission Jesus came to accomplish. Until then it was hidden from them. From that day on, they understood Jesus' kingdom. From then on, they began to establish it and preached the gospel of that kingdom everywhere they went.

Even the disciples expected and believed that Jesus was going to restore a natural kingdom to Israel after His resurrection. Many times they had asked Him about it and made special recommendations about who should be sitting and ruling with Him (Matthew 20:21; Acts 1:6).

Every time Jesus told them about His death, saying He would be leaving them after His resurrection, they were not happy to hear it. One of His closest disciples, Peter, tried to influence Him to change His mind about going to the cross. The Bible says Peter rebuked Jesus and told Him openly that it should never happen to Him. Imagine a disciple trying to rebuke Jesus (Matthew 16:22)! Jesus called him Satan because the thoughts Peter had were inspired by Satan.

Keep in mind that this happened before the death and resurrection of Jesus Christ. The disciples did not understand that Jesus' mission was global: He did not come just to restore the nation of Israel. He came to save the whole world. He still wants His mission and the message of the kingdom to reach the uttermost parts of the earth.

Is God against believers becoming political leaders in nations today? The answer is a big no. Is God against a believer becoming a prime minister or the president of a nation? No. Is God against a believer in Christ starting a multi-national company? No. Not if it is His will and plan. There is no scripture in the New Testament that says we should not become influencers of politics or community. Instead we should strive for it and train our children to be kings and queens on earth because the Bible says when the righteous are in authority people rejoice (Proverbs 29:2).

I strongly believe there are believers who are anointed to be in such positions, but they are not trained or released to do it yet. The Holy Spirit is hoping to accomplish this through all these teachings about the kingdom of God. As the body of Christ receives them, the seeds for these ministries will grow in fertile soil in those called to be in these positions. When they are mature, those people will walk into those places in the nations of the world.

As I wrote in my previous books, we need to witness Jesus as King, Lord, and Judge, and not simply as Healer, Prophet, and Teacher, in this day and age. Believers have to be in places of influence and should be better in all they put their hand to in comparison to the ungodly. We should be the most productive people on the face of the earth because we are the salt and light of the earth, and children of the Most High God.

When Jesus told His disciples that He was going to Jerusalem, they thought He was going there to proclaim Himself as King and establish His throne. In the spiritual sense, He did. He fulfilled the prophecy of Zechariah, in which he said their king was coming riding on a donkey (Zechariah 9:9). The people were filled with great joy when He rode into Jerusalem. They were ecstatic. Jesus was compelled to share another parable to make it clear to them that He was not going there to establish His kingdom, but to die. He explained it all, but they could not comprehend it until later. Below is one of the final parables Jesus shared just before He went to Jerusalem.

> Now as they heard these things, He spoke another parable, because He was near Jerusalem and because they thought the kingdom of God would appear immediately. Therefore He said: "A certain nobleman went into a far country to receive for himself a kingdom and to return. So he called ten of his servants, delivered to them ten minas and said to them, 'Do business till I come.' But his citizens hated him, and sent a delegation after him, saying, 'We will not have this man to reign over us.'
>
> And so it was that when he returned, having received the kingdom, he then commanded these servants, to whom he had given the money, to be called to him, that he might know how much every man had gained by trading. Then came the first, saying, 'Master, your mina has earned ten minas.' And he said to him, 'Well done, good servant; because you were faithful in a very little, have authority over ten cities.' And the second came, saying, 'Master, your mina has earned five minas.' Likewise he said to him, 'You also be over five cities.'
>
> Then another came, saying, 'Master, here is your mina, which I have kept put away in a handkerchief. For I feared you, because you are an austere man. You collect what you did not deposit, and reap what you did not sow.' And he said to him, 'Out of your own mouth I will judge you, you wicked

servant. You knew that I was an austere man, collecting what I did not deposit and reaping what I did not sow. Why then did you not put my money in the bank, that at my coming I might have collected it with interest?'

And he said to those who stood by, 'Take the mina from him, and give it to him who has ten minas.' (But they said to him, 'Master, he has ten minas.') For I say to you, that to everyone who has will be given; and from him who does not have, even what he has will be taken away from him. But bring here those enemies of mine, who did not want me to reign over them, and slay them before me'" (Luke 19:11-27).

This parable is a practical teaching about what the church should be doing right now. Jesus did not tell us to wait for a revival to come, or to hang in there until He came to get us out of here. No. He told us to do business until He comes. The King James Translation says, "Occupy till I come." A major part of the body of Christ has neglected this teaching. Instead they have been waiting for the evacuation.

I believe you have been blessed by reading this book. You may have to read it more than once to receive everything in it. Read it and study it until it becomes part of you. Use it for Bible study groups and teach others. When you teach something it helps you learn better. To order more copies, please visit www.KingdomNetwork.org

May the Holy Spirit open our eyes as He did for the disciples. Let us fill the entire earth with the knowledge of His glory. Let us work together as one body to bring our King back to reign on earth. God bless you.

More Books & Resources

DISCIPLING NATIONS SERIES

Kingdom Mandate (for any donation)
Discovering the Lost Kingdom (Volume 1) $14.00
Purpose, Calling, and Gifts (Volume 2) $15.00
God's Original Design (Volume 3) $20.00
Seeing, Entering, and Manifesting the Kingdom of God (Volume 4) $20.00
The Ekklesia (Volume 5) $30.00
The Gospel of the Kingdom (Volume 6) $20.00
Power and Authority of the Church (Volume 7) $15.00
Kingdom Family (Volume 8) $15.00
The Birthing of a kingdom nation (Volume 9) $20.00
What happened to God (Volume10) $20.00
7 Dimensions and Operations of the Kingdom of God (Volume 11) $15.00
Kingdom Economy (Volume 12) $15.00
Kingdom Government (Volume 13) $15.00
Releasing Kings and Queens to their Original Intent (Volume 14) $10.00
Kingdom Secrets to Restoring Nations Back to God (Volume 15) $20.00

KINGDOM LIVING SERIES

The Three Most Important Decisions of Your Life $15.00
Keys to Passing Your Spiritual Tests $15.00
Recognizing God's Timing for Your Life $12.00
Overcoming the Spirit of Poverty $10.00
Seven Kinds of Believers $10.00
7 Dimensions of God's Glory $5.00
7 Dimensions of God's Grace $10.00
7 Kinds of Faith $7.00

KINGDOM BOOKS FOR KIDS

Genesis 126 Three Volume Book set for boys $25.00

TO PLACE AN ORDER:

www.TheKingdomNetwork.org
Phone: 1-800-558-5020
Email: info@TheKingdomNetwork.org

Are you struggling to discover your **PURPOSE ?**
You are not supposed to fit in but stand out !

Sign up today for the upcoming
FREE Online Kingdom Course

DISCOVERING

THE LOST KINGDOM

In this course you'll DISCOVER:

›› Your true identity and purpose
›› What God is doing on the earth and how you can partner with Him in it
›› Why God created the earth and put us on this planet
   And much more ...

Why are people becoming more and more disinterested in **church and religion** globally?
Join the course, and discover **what your soul has been searching for all along.**

FREE BOOK AND STUDY GUIDE

other courses available
›› DISCOVERING PURPOSE, CALLING AND GIFTS
›› SEEING, ENTERING AND MANIFESTING THE KINGDOM
›› GOD'S ORIGINAL DESIGN | FEBRUARY 2024
›› The Ekklesia
›› The Next move of GOD
   And more ...

Register Now @ **www.TheKingdomUniversity.org**